Will I Ever Love Again?

Memoirs of a Broken-Heart

Na-Tasha Rise

Will I Ever Love Again? Memoirs of a Broken-Heart
Copyright © 2021 by Na-Tasha Rise

All rights reserved—This book is protected by the copyright laws of the United States of America. This book may not be copied or reprinted for commercial gain or profit. No part of this publication may be reproduced in whole or in part, distributed, or transmitted in any form or by any means, including photocopying, recording, or other electronic or mechanical methods, without written permission of the author and/or publisher, except in the case of brief quotations embodied in critical reviews and specific non-commercial uses permitted by the copyright law. It is encouraged and permitted to use short quotations for personal or group study purposes. For information regarding permission, write to Na-Tasha Rise, PO Box 1856, Rincon, GA 31326.

Scripture quotations are taken from the Kings James Version (KJV), New International Version (NIV), The Good News Translation (GNT), The Message Bible (MSG), Contemporary English Version (CEV), The Passion Translation (TPT), New Living Translation (NLT), and the Holy Bible: Easy to Read Version (ERV), Public Domain.

Published by Gift From Above Publishing
501 Lisa St Suite 7A
Rincon, GA 31326

ISBN 978-0-578-31454-9

Cover Design: Jeffrey (Jaebars) Townsell

Printed in the USA.

Acknowledgment

There is no point in going forward with *"Will I Ever Love Again?"* if I don't acknowledge the one where my help comes from. The one who has blessed me with the opportunity to write this book in the first place. The Almighty Lord-the Father, Lord Jesus-the Savior, and the Holy Spirit, I thank You for all You have done for me. I am nothing without You. Lord, my creator, my beginning and end, You have kept me through this journey and have downloaded the words on these pages. Thank You, Jesus, for loving all your children and me.

I must thank and acknowledge the men and women of Unwavering Faith International Outreach Ministries (UFIO). Those 5 am prayers are the truth.

"Get all the advice and instruction you can, so you will be wise the rest of your life. You can make many plans, but the Lord's purpose will prevail."
~Proverbs 19:20-21 (NLT)

My Sister-Friends are the absolute best. I want to thank the women of UFIO's P.U.S.HinG Ministry; My Red Cross Relief Team; who has pulled me out of life's most horrific ruts. Thank you, ladies, for interceding with me and for me while the Lord purged and pruned every weed out of my garden. The journey continues, and I'm humbly grateful God placed you all in my life. You ladies have helped me, guided me, and most importantly, loved me with all my flaws. Indeed, you are my Sisters Keepers.

I am giving thanks to my daughter, Xzasha. Oh, how Mommy loves you so. Babygirl, continue to make Mommy proud. I cry tears of joy while watching you transform into a fearless woman of God. Going through life is worth it because I have you.

I am giving thanks to my family for their continuous words of encouragement. Those daily FaceTime calls bring me life. Love you with all my heart.

To Jeffrey, my graphic designer, photographer, and encourager, you bring new insight to my visions. Thank you for seeing it and helping me to bring them forth. You are God sent... Thank You!

Table of Contents

Foreword 7
Introduction 8
POEM: WOMAN 2 WOMAN 12
Denial 14
POEM: I AM NOT DENIED 20
POEM: NEVER LET GO 22
Prayer 24
Suffering 26
POEM: LETTER FROM THE FATHER 33
POEM: WHAT CAN SEPARATE ME? 35
Prayer 37
Anger 38
POEM: MAD WOMAN 46
POEM: SHATTERING THE NORM 47
Prayer 48
Bargaining 50
POEM: BARGAIN WITH WHO? 57
POEM: I WILL NEVER FORGET YOU 59
Prayer 61
Dying 63
POEM: NEAR-DEATH 72

My Revelation	74
Note to Reader	75
Deliverance Prayer	76
Guilt	78
POEM: INTENTIONAL	84
POEM: SHE IS	85
Prayer	87
Depression	89
POEM: KILLING ME SOFTLY	95
Acceptance	97
POEM: BREAKTHROUGH	101
Prayer	103
POEM: WHAT DOES FREEDOM	104
Will I Ever Love Again?	106
Judgement Day	113
My Revelation	118
POEM: ARE YOU WILLING	120
HEARTFELT THANK-YOU	122
POEM: THE MOTHER OF MANY	125
About the Author	127

Foreword

When I read the pages of this book, I was intrigued. It spoke volumes about uplifting one another and self; as a unity with respect and dignity—women encouraging and empowering women, a village – a sisterhood.

Words can impact an individual, and these words I have engulfed while reading, **Will I Ever Love Again?** I went on a journey with a woman I have known her whole life but am genuinely just getting to understand and admire her. I'm learning the little things I have instilled in her have grown into something bigger than I could ever imagine. She has kept God first in everything she is doing, and she is now encouraging other Beautiful Blessed Queens to do the same.

You are not alone!

Your best support system is God. Put God first! You can do all things through Christ, who gives you the utmost strength. Women don't have to tear each other down, so many are going through the same things. Wow! All of this has come to light for me, and I am blessed to hear it from my very own sweet daughter.

To my beautiful, blessed daughter, I positively admire the woman you have become. I respect your strength, your drive, and your perseverance. Continue to keep our Lord and Savior Jesus Christ at the forefront of your life, and the blessings will overflow. Keep lifting your voice, empowering others to do the same. I love you more than anything.

Your Mother

Introduction

One of the hardest things I ever did was walk away from my marriage. My husband did no wrong, but his love was not the crazy love I was expecting. The love I've always longed for. Through this journey, I've come to realize that my husband was blinded, just as I have been. The only difference between us was I was willing to see – I knew there was better if I could just see me as God sees me. When I met him, I was a product of the world --- broken, hurt, confused, and was looking for someone to love me with all my flaws. Truthfully, I was looking for a savior, but I found out that I was looking for it in the wrong place.

I'm so grateful for marrying my husband; it has done the most remarkable thing for me; it PUSHed me into purpose. Things started to not feel right in my second year of marriage, even though we had been together by this time seven years, so I did the only thing I knew how to do; I began to pray. During my fourth year of marriage, I had started to partake in a prayer line. Six days a week at 5 am, a change took place like never before because of my dedication on the line. I was beginning to think God wasn't hearing me because I was still caught in the world but fighting awfully hard to "live" right. I thought it wasn't enough. Only to my surprise, the most remarkable thing happened. He spoke to me. I mean, God really talked to me… My heart dropped, and that's when I knew I was welcomed and loved by God.

My dreams for my husband and me began to fade, he loved me, which I knew, but I quickly realized that his love for me was to his standards and not of God's. I held him in a place that he didn't earn, and frankly, he never belonged there, to begin with.

Often, we get into relationships and place our partners on these pedestals they shouldn't be on. We put them before everything, and that's not correct. We worship the ground they walk on, and that's not correct. I'm not saying that we shouldn't honor, respect, and cherish them, just as God desires us to love and cherish ourselves. Still, no man should be before God and your God-given destiny.

> *"You must worship no other gods, for the Lord, whose very name is Jealous, is a God who is jealous about His relationship with you."*
>
> ~Exodus 34:4 (NLT)

> *"So, every married man should be gracious to his wife just as he is gracious to himself. And every wife should be tenderly devoted to her husband."*
>
> ~Ephesians 5:33 (TPT)

God desires for us to be loved and spread love amongst others. But we should be so careful not to put others before our own life, the life God destined for us to have.

I'm no expert on relationships, and I don't have a Master's nor a Ph.D. in Marriage Counseling. But there are a few things I've learned along the way that's vital to my story.

1. You are never alone.
2. I am my Sister's Keeper, so what I share with you may help your own life.

3. We are a community of love, peace, and joy; therefore, I will share it, live it, and rejoice in it.

I pray that reading this book can give you insight, strength, and perseverance to endure a separation or divorce process. If you are separated, please ensure you have done all you can to save your marriage, especially if that's your heart's desire. I'm not telling anyone to divorce if it's not necessary because if I could have, I would still be married to my husband.

I separated from the man I loved and adored more than anything for over one year and realized his love could never compare to what I was worth. I believe individuals can find unconditional love even when there are moments when you want to "chop your partner in the throat" (Figuratively). Smile, laughter is good for the soul. Even when you have those frustrating moments in your relationship, I believe communication, compassion, and faith can carry those relationships through. I lacked communication and support in my house. No means to an understanding – and that's where the end of my love story began.

During my separation, prayer was the only thing that kept me going besides God's women in my life. Women after His own heart and their words of encouragement kept me sane. Joy came from communing with God, my daughter, and my Sister-Friends daily. They were the only reasons I got up every morning. I thanked God for breathing life into me each day. I prayed for strength to continue showing my daughter with faith in God that you can overcome anything. I lavished on the friendship and love He created in my life.

I began to journal my emotions, feelings, revelations because I knew this journey in my life would lead to a spiritual breakthrough. At this point, I was so tired of being in my life but not living my life; a change had to happen.

I knew God to be a healer, restorer, mind-regulator, deliverer, and provider. I knew Him to be understanding, so since He was all these things to me, Am I really living for Him? When I questioned myself, "What does God mean to me?" My thoughts seemed to run wildly. Then I asked God, Why me? Am I worthy of living honorably in You? Amongst other questions I've asked, His response was so profound, *"You were created in my image. I gave you life and life more abundantly. I am God, who reigns over the just as well as the unjust. I am a Father who welcomed you into the house of the beloved. You are the daughter of a King; therefore, I have given you power and authority to speak to mountains, and it shall be moved."*

At that very moment, I cried... I no longer felt like an orphaned child. I lifted my head, raised my arms, and prayed that supernatural strength would take me over because this would be a bumpy ride, and I knew it. When it was all over, I also knew my freedom would be waiting for me on the other side.

As Tasha Cobbs Leonard wrote, this is the freedom I have been waiting for... I'm stepping into the joy of the Lord and welcoming my blessed season.

Woman 2 Woman

I'm talking to you this day.
There is a lot I need to say.
I need to empower, encourage, and elevate.
So, it is no longer anything to debate.

Woman 2 Woman, I'm saying to you.
You are uniquely created, better than the mist in the morning dew.
Your presence means the world to me,
And my love stretches farther than the big blue sea.
Together we stand, divided we fall,
So, unity is how we get through any obstacles at all.

Why would I tear you down?
When we were created to be unified.
Why should I rejoice in your success?
'Cause I am my Sisters Keepers.
Love, Unity, and Peace bring joy like no other.
Your kids are mine, mine is yours, and we are all their mothers.
Look at me, as the sister that I am,
Helping you to rebuild your castle with the most precious gems.

Woman 2 Woman, I'm there for you,
And frankly, we can use each other to fight for that ultimate breakthrough.

Grace and Mercy is part of the plan,
And the Blood of Jesus is our guardsman.
Encourage, empower, and elevate to another level.
While we are there together, we can defeat the enemy, any and all,
    especially king devil, the meanest of them all.

So, Woman 2 Woman, I say to you,
There are so many we can accomplish,
When it's more than just me and you.
Let me help you fix your crown,
And pick you up off the ground.
And when I have moments when I am down,
Please, my dear sister, help me fix my crown.

Woman 2 Woman, I'm saying to you,
You are uniquely created, better than the mist of the morning dew.
Together we stand, divided we fall,
So, unity is how we will get through any obstacles at all.

Denial

My heart is grievously pained within me, and the terrors of death have fallen upon me. Fear and trembling have come upon me; horror and fright have overwhelmed me.

Psalms 55:4-5 (AMPC)

Denial:
The refusal to accept the facts of a loss, either consciously or unconsciously. (WebMd.com)

Here is a perfect definition of denial because I refused to accept losing my marriage. I wanted to make it work. I wanted to see, maybe just maybe, what I heard and saw in my dreams was incorrect. The vision of how I saw my life began to shift, and it scared the living hell out of me. It scared me so bad; I started pleading with my husband for two years, "something has to change; we can't keep living like this." At first, I didn't understand what that meant until May 2019, I had the worst dream of my life, and the message was "separate." That message was wrong on all levels, not my marriage, not the man I love, and my only response was, "No, not until you tell me why!" God, I got married so I can live right. I got married so I can honor you, and you can bless me. I got married because it made me whole. I got married because society says so. When I look back and think about my life and the situations and events that led to my marriage, I was all wrong. Even though I married for the right reason, love, I never got consent from my Heavenly Father to marry my husband. Even on my wedding day, before he gave me away, my Daddy told my husband, "If you marry my Daughter, it will cost you." We laughed, but he was right. Marrying me was going to cost, and neither my husband nor I knew the extent of that cost.

2020, Ten days before my birthday, I was going through life, still confused at how things were panning out, even having dreams and visions of weights shackled to my feet, weighing me down. I had to move. I was stifled but had no idea where I would even begin until one day, a mighty word hit me, and it confirmed what I was dreaming. No one knew. I couldn't speak those words to anyone but God! And it was, "If you don't leave, you will surely die." I cried because this couldn't happen to me, not now, not ever. I didn't know what I was going to do. Those words stirred up something within me, and this time I couldn't ignore it. So, I surrendered. I was no longer going to fight another day. My response was now, "*God if this is really You, You got to move on my behalf. I have nothing to move with and nowhere to go. I'm trusting You right now with all of me.*" Can I tell you when you stay in the vein and stay at God's feet, leaving it all at the altar so that He can deal with it? God pumps life into a bad situation.

Five days before my birthday, I was singing with my church praise team, and while in the pulpit, God showed me a woman. She was praising God, and the Holy Spirit spoke, ***"Ask her if she is looking for a roommate."*** I was in total awe just hearing Him talk, right there in front of the congregation. I was praying no one saw the tears that began streaming down my face. I heard Him clearer than I have ever before, and I knew at that very moment I was in the presence of the King. After service, I was contemplating asking this woman whom I barely knew this question. Still, I was obedient, and the response I received blew my mind even more. Yes, she was. I screamed and danced the whole way home. When I entered my house, it hit me. I really had to go. The enemy was lurking because my husband and I disagreed that evening. The tension was already in the house, and it rose higher than ever before. As the songwriter, Nelly, wrote, "It's getting hot in here." The heat had been turned up. I had the go-ahead but still denied the power thereof. I didn't want to go, even if it meant my life.

I cried the whole night. I tossed and turned, and just as I finally fell asleep, I heard a knock on the door. I jumped up only to find no one was there. Then I heard the voice again, ***"I'm knocking. Are you going to let me in?"*** The door of opportunity opened, and I had to take it. That night, I was reading 1 Kings 1:1-4, and what came to mind was, "Can you lie in a dead situation and still live?" The dream of the chains shackled at my feet came back to me, the word of life or death came back to me, and I knew I had to take the opportunity which presented itself to me. The next day, I called the young woman to confirm if she was looking for a roommate, and she still was. I moved the same day.

Talking to the Boss:

Thank you, Abba Father.

Ok, Boss! You must have a trick up your sleeve because all the emotions I'm feeling right now are unreal. I thank you for all that You have done in my life. I'm thankful for the relationship that we have developed, Father. I am after Your heart, Father, but I must ask, why are you taking me to this place of uncertainty? I have no extra finances. I have my car note, insurance, my Daughter's tuition, my tuition. How am I going to survive? I don't make enough to cover my expenses. I thought education was my profession; I made a career change in my mid 30's, I didn't even finish school yet. Are you sure this is the right time? I can't deal with this, God, not right now. Is this in actuality happening? This transition can't be real.

Thank you, Abba Father, for introducing me to you before the tornado arrived. Since I've always been fascinated with weather, I've compared my grieving to a tornado.

Insight: Wedge Tornado – broader and wider, which makes it more dangerous and destructive. The damage done by these storms is sometimes hard to replace.

So, Father, Thank you for the Rope Tornado. Though it's slender and sleek, damage and strife were caused, but the impact is repairable. Gracious am I for the Red Cross Relief Team you surrounded me with to resuscitate me. Sometimes I feel I skipped the denial stage of grieving. Then, the realization hit me. I have been grieving for two years before I finally obeyed your voice. I was in denial that I wouldn't be anything without my counterpart. I was in denial that life would be worthless without my "king." I began to realize there is life after death.

Many say separation or divorce is like death. You are losing something so significant in your life. Even though your spouse is still alive, he is dying subliminally. Death, defined to me, is the separation of person, place, or thing physically, mentally, and/or spiritually. It affects every aspect of your thought process. Experts state denial is a coping mechanism that protects you by numbing the hurt or pain's impact. Honestly, as I began to go through, the tears that started to fall could never amount to the peace and joy within myself I desperately wanted to hold on to. God granted me the strength and courage to leave, so I'm sure He would grace me with the same power and authority to go through.

I must go to it for me to go through it, and that's where my victory awaits me.

I am the Daughter of a King, the Most High King at that. I am royalty, and my "king," the one who God places in my life to support me, love me, and cover me, would see himself as such. WORTHY! He would also acknowledge himself as a son in the house of royalty. He would see himself as a Man of Valor, a Demon Slayer, or even a Kingdom Warrior. He will be confident in the power and authority he will possess. This man would put fear in the enemy's heart just by looking at him. We would be able to stand the test of time. No demon in hell would want to come near our dwelling place. Now that may be far-fetched, but the man that God places in my life must love God just as I do. So, I'm thanking you in advance for what lies ahead. I will continue to honor and respect my husband until my time comes, but I must continue to believe there is life after death.

Thank you, Father, for having my back. Thank you for walking alongside me in the face of adversity. Thank you for downloading an action plan for me to accept being gracefully broken.

I Am Not Denied

Fear once struck my heart,
How can I go and leave all I've known behind?
Just to hear you tell me, I am not worthy,
And I wouldn't be granted God's mercy.

Oh My! Fear had stricken my heart,
But God's courage has jumped and made it restart.
God spoke of giving me strength when I am weak,
He says I am the woman He's called me to be; if it's Him, I seek.
Yes, If I only believe, then my life can be redeemed.
God says, His Love conquers all.
Therefore, I've been welcomed into the house of the beloved.
I Am Not Denied.

Fear once struck my heart,
No finances, nowhere to go, I wouldn't know where to start.
Just to hear you tell me, I am not worthy,
And I wouldn't be made whole.
That I would fall and whither into a black hole.

Fear had stricken my heart,
But God's courage has jumped and made it restart.
God says love is patient, and love is kind,
He said that I would be healed within time.
His love conquers all.
Therefore, I'm welcomed into the house of the beloved.
I Am Not Denied.

The enemy thought he had me,
When he struck my heart with fear.
But what he failed to believe is.
My God said, "I'm His," and He holds me near.
His Daughter, a royal priesthood,

Welcomed into the house of the beloved.
So, the enemy shall surely fail.
No weapon formed against me shall prosper,
His love conquers all,
Therefore, I hold my head high.
I am loved by the Most High...
I Am Not Denied.

The enemy is the liar of lies;
he has caused many tears, I've cried,
Now his lies will surely die because I chose to stay alive.

I AM NOT DENIED.

Never Let You Go!

There is nothing that you can do to ever make me leave your side.
I am truly that 'ride or die.'
My heart understands the love and loyalty of your heart.
My heart welcomes you with open arms,
Though we've experienced many false alarms.

My heart and love are so genuine that I will never leave you or forsaken you.
So, what must I do to keep you here with me?
Can't you see that I will never leave, and I desire you to be with me.
There is nothing you can do to ever make me leave your side,
Like I said before I am that 'ride or die.'

You can run from me, but you can't hide,
I will always be there to pick you up off the ground, dust you off,
and remove the grave mound.
There is not enough drugs, abuse, or alcohol in the world,
To stop me from loving my favorite girl.

You are precious to me and this you must see,
That no one will truly understand the way your life is planned out for you,
But me.

There are some who can embrace you.
There are some who will try to chase you.
There are some who will connect to the mystery that comes from deep within.

But there are many who just don't want to see you win.
But that's where I come in.

I give you strength when you are weak,
And authority comes from your mouth every time you speak.
Life is grand because you are here,
You are to me, my Lumiere.

My love for you is loyal,
And this is what I need the world to see,
Just how much you really mean to me.

The creation of you has been done with such perfection.
Even though, you thought you wanted to make some corrections.
And in the midst of that, some errors have been made.
But my reflection of you has never changed.

Hold on to my love and my faithfulness,
You will need it for the ride.
The transformation is beginning,
And you heart is being purified.
There is nothing you could ever do to make me stop loving you.
So, allow me to rest within you,
Speak to you, eat with you, and dream with you.

Because you are my special love,
and I will never let you go.

Prayer

Father God, In the Name of Jesus,

I lift up women this day. The many women that are like me, carrying the weight and burdens of death. Death from a divorce, a breakup, or even a physical death. Allow these women to believe that the power that lies within is mightier and more potent than they could imagine. We are Women of God, Daughters of a King. We are courageous enough to launch into the deep with you. With assurance, we would not drown.

I pray, Father God, that you wrap your loving arms around us as we begin to deal with the trial that lies ahead. Separation/ Divorce is like death; we are losing a significant part of our being. So, Father, I ask that you fill every vacant place with love, peace, and joy. With what we are about to encounter, I pray we take this time to do a self-assessment and draw closer to you.

Father, I pray that we would not deny ourselves our identity for the sake of someone else. We would understand our worth. I pray for healing over our minds, bodies, and souls. I pray that you grant us wisdom, knowledge, and understanding for a strategy on how to pick up the broken pieces of our lives, so we may be able to start anew.

Prayer

Father, I pray for those that desire to reconcile, that you restore and build communication in their household, so the cords of love can continue to blossom. No matter the outcome, Father, I pray that your will be done in our lives.

Give us the serenity to accept the things we cannot change,
Change the things that we can.
And grant us the wisdom to know the difference.

Father, Let Your Will Be Done!

In Jesus Name,
Amen!

Suffering

He will wipe every tear from their eyes, and there will be no more death or sorrow or crying or pain. All these things are gone forever.

Revelation 21:4 (NLT)

Suffering:
The state of undergoing pain, distress, or hardship. (Dictionary.com)

The bible states that the Lord heals the brokenhearted and bandages their wounds (Psalms 147:3, NLT). If so, God, why does it feel like you are not here with me? Why do I feel like my heart has been ripped out of my chest? Will I ever breathe again?

For days, I have been going through agonizing pain; the tears have not been able to stop falling. Every time I think about you, I cry. I can't even answer your call because I cried and there is no other explanation, but I AM HURT... I don't know what to do, I know I heard you, Lord, and I was obedient to your voice, so why am I so hurt? I didn't think it would be like this. I didn't know I would cry, but then again, why wouldn't I? You are my Love. You meant the world to me, so I should assume pain and hurt were attached to me leaving. I went to bed at night in distress, and if I could get any sleep at all, I woke up tired and depressed. I was in a place that was not my home. It was not the home I intended to have, nor the house I started to create and build. I wanted what was mine, and it made me mournful I couldn't have it. What hurt me the most was, there was no attempt to ensure I was welcomed back.

Days turned into months, and I felt more heavyhearted than I've ever been before in my life. Suddenly, I realized I needed to get out of this rut. I didn't know how much longer I could pretend in public I was fine, but deep down in my heart, all I did was cry. I was still in love, even though he didn't love me back. I still cared, even though he didn't care that much for me. I tried to be there whenever I was needed, but I felt nothing had changed to no avail. Communication had become a barrier that became harder to break. Boy, does this thing hurt?

One day, while wallowing in my hurt and pain. I was meditating on the Verse of the Day that I stumbled upon in my email. It read, **"Create in me a clean heart, O God, and renew a steadfast spirit within me" (Psalms 51:10, NKJV).** God sure knows how to get our attention when He wants us to listen, and when we are in the position to receive, He speaks even louder. During my meditation, I heard the words, **"what is the condition of your heart?"** At first, I didn't understand, but as I continued to read Psalms 51:10, I realized my heart's condition was becoming toxic.

Anyone that endures some type of suffering, if not careful, will begin to harbor other ailments. Ailments like bitterness, anger, resentment, amongst many other conditions we can possess. The question quickly becomes, can we give all our hurt, pain, and distress to God so He may be able to deal with it for us? Can we trust God enough to help us through it all? Are we willing to forgive, even ourselves, to begin the process of healing?

I realized that God talked to me through my tears, hurt, pain, and distress on this day. He wanted to create a clean heart in me. He wanted me to realize that my heart's conditions would lead to what my spiritual life will entail. If my heart hurts, then I speak hurtful things. Would I be effective in healing myself, let alone another, if I were living conducive to the pain and brokenness that lies in my heart? God is love, and there is no love in hurt and pain. On this day, I made the conscious, deliberate decision to release feelings of resentment or vengeance toward the man I loved, regardless of whether he deserved it or not. I asked God to help me to forgive. I was not making excuses or condoning any offenses towards me or to myself. I was allowing myself the peace of mind and freedom from the hurt, pain, bitterness, just to name a few emotions I was currently going through, to be unclogged from my mind. My thought process needed to change so my heart process could begin to heal.

God said, **"Don't be conformed to the world and be renewed by the transforming of my mind" (Romans 12:2)**. I wanted God to heal my heart, so I had to reform my thinking. Think as Jesus think, Love like Jesus loved, and I would be healed like only Jesus can heal. Now daily, I ask myself, *"What is the condition of my heart?"* Then I tell the Lord, *"If there is anything in my heart that is not conducive to your love, please forgive me, Father, and remove it from me, please. I don't want to do anything to push me out of your will because I know I can't make it through this thing called life without You."*

Talking to the Boss:

Thank you, Abba Father, for teaching me how to forgive. Thank you for being the healer I need in my life. Thank you for speaking to me even in my suffering, letting me know you are right there with me through it all.

I never realized my unhappiness until I had to face it. I was suffering long before I began to see it. I hid behind the superwoman persona. I gave this man whom I loved all of me. I needed him to save me from myself. I needed it so much; I allowed it, the hurt me, to make decisions in my life that were not conducive to my destiny. In my suffering, You, Father, allowed me to look at the woman in the mirror and accept my faults in my marriage and my own life.

I walked around like a superwoman for many years, burying the hurt, pain, abuse, misunderstanding, and addictions. I planted them so deep that another persona was developed to protect them. "She" would stop at nothing to ensure I was not hurt. "She" shoveled up the mess and stuck it deep into my heart, so deep not even I could reach it. But God! There was someone who could, and His name is Jesus. In my suffering, He started plucking, and picking, and uprooting all that "She" hid. This was the beginning of my new life. This was the beginning of my destiny.

> *But that's not all! We gladly suffer, because we know that suffering helps us to endure. And endurance builds character, which gives us a hope that will never disappoint us. All of this happens because God has given us the Holy Spirit, who fills our hearts with His Love. ~Romans 5:3-5 (CEV)*

After reading this, Oh My! My heart dropped with excitement. Here I am about to believe the enemy that it's ok to stay in this broken place feeling worthless, hurt, and angry. I almost agreed with all that the enemy said about me. But look how my Father decides to uplift me by letting me know this is just a phase. I don't belong here. He's only building character and endurance for the journey that lies ahead. Look at how my Father reminds me there is still hope. Hope in Love, Hope in life, and Hope in happiness.

No matter the suffering we encounter in our life, whether it's death, separation, divorce, misunderstandings, or rejection, whatever it is… After we get over the initial hurt, we must be willing to face the sting of the blow. Everything we go through, no matter how big or small, is a test of our faith. It may seem complicated but remember that everything the enemy meant for evil God works together for His glory (Romans 8:28). The victory belongs to Him. God sent His son Jesus to Earth so that He could be the ultimate sacrifice. The lamb that died on the cross for our iniquities. Then, Jesus endured the suffering and still made the conscious decision to stay there and watch the promises of God come through. He rose, giving us (God's children) power and authority to cast away all the enemy throws our way (Just think, since we are God's children, we are like Jesus' siblings, WOW!). So, you see, the enemy could never break us unless we authorize him to do so. We must be willing to face the "sting of the blow" because it is meant to build our endurance and character during this journey called life.

In our place of suffering, we must remember,

"Sometimes, it's the journey that teaches you a lot about your destination."

Drake

Where are you going from here? We can't forget there is a purpose for our lives. We must continue to push through the pain, hurt, bitterness to see what's on the other side. We must continue to go through the valley and see what the light entails. In the light, our purpose is revealed.

Also, we are reminded that,

"Peace is a journey of a thousand miles, and it must be taken one step at a time."

Lyndon B. Johnson

No matter how hard it gets,
we must be willing to get up and take that one step.

"In the midst of every crisis lies great opportunity."

Albert Einstein

Allow God the opportunity, and He will surely give you rest.

"Even when their paths wind through the dark valley of tears, they dig deep to find a pleasant pool where others find only pain. He gives to them a brook of blessing filled from the rain of an outpouring."
~Psalms 84:6 (TPT)

"God, your wraparound presence is our defense. In your kindness, look upon the faces of your anointed ones.
~Psalms 84:9 (TPT)

Letter From the Father

To my daughter,

I see your pain.
I know just what you are going through.
I am here with you
I know all about your crazy thoughts and messy emotions,
'cause I am here with you.
I don't require you to have it all together,
'cause I am here with you.
I offer comfort in your sorrow and displeasures,
'cause I am here with you.

I see your pain; I see your tears…
I'll make you laugh, smile, and love again,
If you just believe.
I love you unconditionally, my daughter.
You are my heart.
I have created you to be one with me from the very start.
I see you in your pain, and I want to make it stop,
but first, you must allow me into your heart.

I know what you're going through, my daughter,
I want you to see,
I can remove every disappointment,
Just trust in me.
I want your heart; just let me have it.
I won't tear it apart 'cause I can't stand to.
I want your heart 'cause you are a part of my soul.
I love you, my daughter, and I want to make you whole.

Do not despair; I am working on your behalf.
You will grow stronger and stronger with every step,
Then you can declare the past is the past,
I won't let it continue to hurt you, over and over again.
When I bring comfort from every sorrow,
Restoration and redemption will surely follow.

My love and kindness are your defense.
I just need you to say, "Jesus, You are my fence."
I see you in your pain,
I see you in your sorrow,
I'm here with you, my daughter,
Walking you through to your Greater Tomorrow.

What can Separate Me?

What can separate me from the love of Christ?
I've asked this question most of my life.
I've buried myself in the hurt and pain,
And I've cried many tears because of the shame.
Then I realized through my sin,
My Father gave His son to the world, so I can win.
Jesus died – so I can stay alive.
To live abundantly prosperous and continue to thrive.
He reigned over the just as well as the unjust,
So, my freedom is a must.
My suffering was so God could get the glory,
While peace and joy pour out during the telling of my story.

My heart has cried for so long,
And through the tears I became strong.
Perseverance, Character and Hope –
God wants to produce in me,
Characteristics that would take me further than the eyes can see.
We must realize our momentary trouble,
Set the angels on guard and they move on the double.

What can separate me from the love of Christ?
Nothing because Jesus already paid the price.
Even when I'm powerless and afraid,
I'm reminded if I prayed,
my life was no longer a charade.
I was fearfully and wonderfully made.
So, through the eyes of my dear Father,
I am His beloved and Precious Daughter.

Prayer

Heavenly Father,

I come before You this day, thanking You for being the Great I Am, thank You for being a Good Father and loving me through the hurt, pain, bitterness, and tears. I thank You, Father, for the peace only You can give while I sit and ravish in Your omniscient presence. The inner peace You have given me during this crucial time in my life is beyond anything I could have ever imagined.

So, Father, I ask for your unconditional love and protection over the hearts and minds of Your children. Release them from worry, fear, anxiety, and all stressors that are not conducive to them living in the fullness of joy for You. I ask for the Gift of Peace over the lives of Your children through their difficult moments. I ask that You help them put on the "Full Armor of God" daily. I ask that You create a clean heart and renew their minds, so they can walk boldly in the battles they face, knowing they are not alone. They know that You, Father, will banish any mountain that stands in the way of their destiny.

Father, I declare peace and joy over your children. No weapons formed against us will prosper, and we will stand on those words. The blood of Jesus has justified us so that nothing can separate us from Your Love.

In Jesus Name,
Amen!

Anger

Refrain from anger and turn from wrath; do not fret-it leads only to evil. For those who are evil will be destroyed, but those who hope in the Lord will inherit the land.

Psalms 37:8-9 (NIV

Anger:
A strong feeling of displeasure and usually of <u>antagonism</u> Antagonism-implication of a natural or logical basis for one's hatred or dislike.
(Merriam-Webster.com)

There is a valid reason for my anger and dislike. Months have gone by, and still nothing from this man I love. We have spoken; I've even assisted in any way that I could but still no words of consolation or reconciliation. The place I've prayed for after we got married and God released into our possession is no longer my home. The residence I was trying to turn into a haven for our family is no longer my home, and it doesn't look like it would ever be. Silence has been the outcome.

The conversation that lit the fuel to the fire was when I knew my marriage was over. *"Can we get counseling?"* I asked. "Why?" was the response I was given sarcastically. "There is nothing wrong." You speak. *"Nothing wrong!"* I yelled. *"What do you mean there is nothing wrong? Your wife is living somewhere else, and you say there is nothing wrong."* His response was so cold it brought fire to my heart. "Yes, that's right. But let me remind my wife she was the one that packed her bag and left. We could have resolved all of her concerns, even with her sleeping in another room of the house." *"What? So, you really believe me sleeping in my daughter's room for three months was going to resolve something."* Rage began building up in my eyes. Flames protruded out of my ears. My heart started to race, and the tears fell, and at that moment, all I could do was cry uncontrollably. My marriage was officially over. I hung up, devastated.

For two years, my life was spiraling out of control. What I thought was my happily ever after became a battle of my respect, dignity, and self-worth. I was living in a house where I wasn't respected. My stepchildren had more control of what happened in my house than I did. If I said clean up, wash the dishes, or maybe pay a damn bill since they were grown. My words fell on deaf ears. Then nothing from "the peanut gallery," he never backed anything I said, even though I was right—no support whatsoever. Maybe it was my upbringing, but no grown child I know can walk into your house and not speak or ignore your greetings. No grown child I know would have had that privilege. My mother probably would have knocked every tooth out of my mouth, and I'm in my forties. It was disheartening to see, I am the woman of my house, and I had to sit, watch, and accept someone else running my house, which had my name on it and all the bills. This is what broke the camel's back.

After our intense conversation, my thoughts began to run wildly. I know I wasn't perfect, but I did everything to ensure my family had everything they needed. I've worked multiple jobs to assist my husband in any financial situation that arose. Mortgage payments, college tuitions, food, transportation, youth league sports, not to mention sleepless nights to ensure we didn't look like what we were going through. So many skeletons lived in our closet, and not even one ever peeped out. And right now, I'm so hurt because this is the thanks I get. My anger increased at the thought of my effortless love and support, only for me to receive his ass to kiss.

I finally fell asleep only to awake an hour and thirty minutes later, trying to get ready for work. I was groggy and miserable, I usually don't call out from work, but this day I couldn't force a smile on my face when my heart was breaking into a million pieces. My eyes were red, my hands were sweaty and shaking, and my body was so hot, I felt like I just came out of a burning furnace. I was going to explode like a grenade.

Then suddenly, BOOM!!!

I screamed. I yelled. I cried.

Why is this happening to me? What did I do to deserve this? I've changed. I've stopped lying, stealing, and cheating. I've even stopped partying and heavy drinking like I used to. A glass of wine, sociably, I figured, wouldn't hurt anybody. I'm not overindulging or getting drunk. I was praying, serving, and worshipping the God that had changed my life. After spending one year with Him, dedicated time to Him, I saw the transformation in my life. I was not the same woman I was. I walked differently, talked differently, and was living differently. My husband had asked this of me, and now he was cross towards me, which I couldn't understand. The more I asked the question, *"Why doesn't he love me?"* The angrier I became. Now, the old Tasha, the street Tasha, the hood Tasha was beginning to speak to me. Her voice was creeping in the angrier I became. She started saying, *"Just go and cut his ass up for disrespecting you, you know how you used to do in the hood? Hell, burn the house down. If you can't live in it, no one should have the opportunity to either. Go ahead and take him for everything he has; you're the half owner of it all, so, technically, it belongs to you anyway. What does he care? He doesn't care about you anyway."* Oh my gosh! The thoughts of wickedness played over and over in my mind, and I cried for hours behind them.

Suddenly, my phone rang. It was one of my prayer sisters. I have such a connection with this older woman of God; I began acknowledging her as my spiritual mother. While speaking to her, I tried to hide the pain in my voice. She asked me to assist her with a project, and I was gathering the information I needed; just when I thought I made it scot-free, she asked one question, "Tasha, What's wrong?" *"Oh nothing, ma, just thinking about going to the beach. I have some work to do."* I said numbly, trying not to sound super fake. "The beach!" she responded questioningly. "Hold on, one minute…." She said quickly. Before I could blink, my other PUSHinG sisters were on the line, and a prayer chain had begun. *"Ma, this is not necessary. I promise it's nothing; the sound of the water can't resolve."*

Against my directives, my PUSHinG sisters prayed anyway, and that's when I entered a place with the Lord I had never been before. The presence of the Lord was so powerful; all I could do was lay out before Him and cry out to Him all the burdens that were weighing my heart down. In a soft whisper, I heard, *"Another level, but do you trust Me? Oh my God, He was speaking to me…"* the tears began to fall. I literally was seeing the chains being pulled down. The chains of anger, bitterness, rejection, resentment, and loneliness were being pulled down. The chains of feeling unworthiness were being broken. The chains of feeling unloved were being crushed. Oh my God! I was being set free right there on the phone. Everything I had on my heart was released before the Lord, and I wanted nothing to do with those feelings ever again. Ten years of being with someone only to find out I wasn't really loved at all. The image of me infatuated this man. He was more obsessed with what I could do for him, not love me and honor me as his wife. If he wanted a roommate, I didn't need to get married for that.

I kept having a reoccurring dream with shackles on my feet. Just to find through revelation, he was the reason I had shackles on my feet. He weighed me down. He was slowing me down from walking into my purpose. Oh my God! Thank you for the revelation. There was so much that was revealed to me on this day. Though, the most important lesson I've learned was how to lay it all at God's feet. I learned how to forgive those who have caused me harm and forgive myself for my thoughts and actions. On this day, I walked into another level in Christ. I had an encounter with God that changed my life forever.

On this hot, muggy Thursday, Natasha Tingman-Orr died, and Na-Tasha Rise had risen from death. I heard the Lord say, *"Now take those grave clothes off and live… You're going to live to see what your destiny is. Your breakthrough is here, and your purpose has surfaced. Now walk into it."*

After hearing such powerful words, my tears dried up and from that day forth. Anger for the man I once loved ceased, and I looked at my situation from a different perspective. I will no longer try to fit into a position God doesn't intend for me to squeeze in but stand out and allow the love and prosperity to come to me. I have favor with the Lord, and there is no lack in Him. Lies and manipulation have no place in my life, and this was the last day I was going to let them control me.

I'm walking into my blessed season!

Talking to the Boss:

Abba Father,

It is a blessing to know I'm loved so much that you will intervene when it is time. You have proven to me time and time again that I am loved and welcomed by You. You have shown me repeatedly that if I trust in you, You will strengthen me in my weakness and help me along the way, on my way to living my blessed life.

> *Fear not [there is nothing to fear], for I am with you; do not look around you in terror and be dismayed, for I am your God. I will strengthen and harden you to difficulties, yes, I will help you; yes, I will hold you up and retain you with My [victorious] right hand of rightness and justice. ~Isaiah 41:10 (AMPC)*

Thank you, Father, for advising me; I have nothing to fear. Even when the enemy tries to plant demented and chaotic thoughts in my mind, You are the God who regulates minds. So, my thoughts are subject to Your words, Your will, and Your way.

> *Who could ever separate us from the endless Love of God's Anointed One? Absolutely, no one! For nothing in the universe has the power to diminish His Love toward us. Troubles, pressures, and problems are unable to come between us and heaven's love. What about persecutions, deprivations, dangers, and death threats? No, for they are all impotent to hinder omnipotent love, ... Yet even in the midst of all these things, we triumph over them all, for God has made us to be more than conquerors, and His demonstrated love is our glorious victory over everything!*
> *~Romans 8:35, 37 (TPT)*

Who could ever separate me from Your unconditional Love? Not anything or anyone! No demon in hell has the power to break me, kill me, or destroy me, even though they may try. There is no burden more tremendous than the Almighty God. So, satan-you lose once again. Life and death lie in my mouth; therefore, I declare I shall live and not die. I will walk into my destiny and fulfill my purpose. I will live the story that was written for my life by my creator. No one can condemn me because Jesus gave His life for me. He conquered death by rising from the grave, exalting the Father, and sitting next to Him on the throne. It's a blessing to know and be reminded Jesus continuously intercedes on my behalf, so there is no trick of the enemy that can't and won't be exposed.

The enemy thought he would have my mind, but he failed to realize my mind is in the submission of my Lord and Savior, Jesus.

Oh, Father God! I'm humbled this day. I sit at your feet, a new creature in you. Accepting my fate in You, not my will, but Your will be done in my life. Lord, thank You for sending your angels to me this day to snatch me out once again from the enemy's hands.

Today, I'm not ashamed to say, I'm nothing without you, Father. If you have not intervened and let the enemy win, I would be in jail for arson, manslaughter, or worse, murder... But God! I must praise You for being the amazing God that You are. You are God all by yourself. You sit high, and you look low, into the secret places and heal the brokenness instantly. The Omniscient God has shown me His favor on this muggy Thursday afternoon, and by His grace and mercy, I've been redeemed.

In Zephaniah 3:17, You said, You sit amongst me, by my side, saving me from all my iniquities and guiding me every step of the way. You surround me with your love, which quiets all my fears and chaotic thoughts, by keeping them under Your submission. While I stay on the altar, feasting off your every word. You will continue to serenade me with songs of sophistication, light-heartedness, love, and grace. In Your arms is where my worth is valued, and I'm reminded of how meaningful I am to you.

There is nothing that can separate me from the Love of You, Jesus!

Thank you, Father, for loving me!
Thank you, Father, for saving me!
Thank you, Father, for deeming me worthy!

I will walk with my head held high in confidence knowing whose daughter I am!
I am the Daughter of a King!

Mad Woman

Ughhh! I'm about to scream!
My heart is beating so fast,
It's pulsating out of my chest.
I'm so consumed with this anger,
It's dictated every breathe I take,
I feel like I'm going to suffocate.

Ughhh! I'm about to scream!
The tears are blinding me.
I can't see through the blood in my eyes.
Lord, save me because I am surely to die.
Call the Ambulance…
Call the Police…
By the time, I'm done,
I'm not going to be the only one who can't breathe.

Where? Why? How could this happen to me?
I've done all I could to transform from the beast to the belle,
But that wasn't enough to prevent me
From having this tragic downfall.
The love of my life, I say.
I've loved with all my heart and soul.
Only for your heart to turn instantly cold.
All because I couldn't live by your ways.
And praise the chaos that began to rule our days.

Then One day, I declared a change and through many tears.
I've surrendered my heart to forgive,
Just as my creator forgave me.
Through this daily process, I began to heal.
Thank you, Jesus, for loving me still.
Many days, I wanted to scream.
I was as mad as mad can be.
But through trusting the man above
I declare I will open my heart once again to love.

Shattering the Norm

Smash! Crack!
My heart has shattered to the floor,
It's broken, misused, and very sore.
It's crying, It's screaming, It's so deformed.
But all I hear You saying,
"I'm shattering the norm."

Breaking the barriers of familiarity.
It will be worth it; it's for your prosperity.
When I say suffer, I need you to crucify.
When I say cry, I need you to let out a war cry.
When I say pray, I need you to pray fervently.
When I say move, I need you to proceed with urgency.
I'm breaking the barriers of familiarity,
And it will be worth it; it's for your prosperity.

My heart has shattered to the floor,
And as I began to clean it up,
You walked through the door.
"What is broken?" You say. "Let it be."
Because I'm shaping and molding you to be
Who I need you to be.
It's time to let go.
It's time to transform.
I'm giving you a new identity,
I've shattered the norm.

Prayer

Father God, I thank you this day for being a patient and understanding Father, slow to anger and slow to speak. You have shown your daughter unconditional love, grace, and kindness through all the hurt, pain, heartaches, and headaches. Since you are slow to anger, I was able to rest in your arms through my temper tantrum as you consoled my crying soul. Father, I thank you for your gentleness, which reminds me how I'm loved, despite what I see or hear through my natural eyes or ears.

Thank you for your daily words of edification and the continuous drawing to my place of purpose. Your Holy words remind me never to seek revenge, for vengeance belongs to You, Father. They also state I will be seen as a fool in Your eyes if I remain angry and judge against those who have harmed me instead of forgiving them, as you have done for me.

Thank you, Father, for daily removing the wrath, malice, anger, and bitterness from my heart. For my mouth pours out the subjects of my heart, and if it's not worthy for your ears Father, they shouldn't be spoken to anyone.

Thank You, Father, for teaching me, downloading in me Your righteous way of living. I desire to please You, and only You, Father. Let Your light shine through the darkness.

    I declare peace over my mind this day. I declare the peace of the Lord over my heart. I will not get upset, frustrated, aggravated over the things I have no control over, and the serenity to deal with the things I can control. No weapon can form against me and prosper. There is no fiery dart in hell that can penetrate the armor of God over my mind, body, and soul. The Spirit of the Lord dwells within me, and His riches and glory will rule and abide above all things. No attack of the enemy can withstand the majestic power of the Lord. The Spirit of the Lord that dwells within me will speak to the mountains, and it shall move. So, I rest assured this day,

        Peace will forever surround me.
        Joy will forever surround me.
        Love will forever surround me.

                                          In Jesus Name,
                                                Amen!

Bargaining

They said to him, "We've come to tie you up and hand you over to the Philistines." Samson said, "Swear to me that you won't kill me yourselves." "Agreed," they answered. "We will only tie you up and hand you over to them. We will not kill you." ....
Judges 15: 12-13 (NIV)

Bargaining:
Bargaining is a line of defense against the emotions of grief. It helps to postpone the sadness, confusion or hurt.

It is not uncommon for religious believers to make a deal or promise with God or a higher power in exchange for healing and relief from grief and pain.
(Healthline.com)

> ***If only you had listened to my commands! Then the blessings would have flowed for you like a stream that never goes dry! Victory would have come to you like the waves that roll on the shore.*** ***~Isaiah 48:18 (GNB)***

I woke up every day this week asking myself this question, could I have been more understanding? What if I ignored my feelings longer? Eventually, I would be able to make decisions in my own home? Couldn't I have continued to ignore the disrespectful, non-supportive behavior from everyone in my house towards me, just to make peace? I could have walked on eggshells just a little bit longer; things would have changed, wouldn't they? Could I have been able to ignore the manipulative, selfish, "me" attitude that sat in the atmosphere? I probably could have just saved my marriage if I did. I probably could have done more to compromise my feelings for the sake of my family. Could I have ignored the thoughts, the pleas, and cries for more communication and support? Could I have dismissed the distance we were having as a couple? Could I have continued to overlook the countless money wasted over the numerous times I tried to rekindle our relationship, only for it to go down the drain in a matter of minutes? When I thought about the vow I made to you before God, I cried inconsolably because my life was spiraling out of control. At first, I couldn't understand why? But now, I'm beginning to believe it was not my destiny at all.

Nothing seemed to work. Counseling was out of the question. Communication was more challenging than I expected. Respect was no longer given, and to top it off, I had to share a home with individuals who thought a clean house was a sin. Maybe if I had listened to the warnings and signs beforehand and ignored what I thought I was feeling, I would have been better off. If I didn't learn anything through this process, I've learned the desires of our heart will be granted and blessed, but it MUST align with God's purpose. We must never move ahead of God, or we will get pushed back to the beginning. Right now, I feel like how I felt when I left my hometown to start anew in another place. I feel like I have nothing and must rebuild my life once again. Jesus! Where do we go from here?

I've been out of my house for six months now, going through the motions of trying to cope with this thing called life. When your heart is attached to an individual in any form, a distance of any type causes hurt. Who would have thought a separation could be so heart-wrenching? I've spent numerous hours replaying the great memories we have shared. The laughs, the hugs, and kisses, the security I felt believing you would never let me down, and it was us against the world. "*Oh, My God!*" I screamed. *"I want it all back. I want my marriage and all it entails. What can I do to get it back? I would do anything to get my life back.*" After I yelled and cried, I asked myself the most complex question, "*Am I walking in God's perfect will if I go back to the way things were? I know God honors marriages, but the marriage is to the man or woman whom He chooses, not you.*" When a man finds a wife, the bible states he finds a good thing (Proverbs 18:22). I sought my husband- he never chased me. At that moment, I realized I made the biggest mistake of my life.

Compared to some, my separation was not so dramatic as other women whose paths I've crossed. My husband was not abusive physically; he was not cheating (even though he had some "friends" I was never fond of). He was a good provider for his family. He did anything to ensure we had, and I was there to support what he couldn't do. So, again I ask why things were so discombobulated in our lives.

Was I selfish? Was I not supportive? Was I the one being disrespectful? Did I allow him to do everything, and I did nothing? I have constantly heard these words from the mouth of the man I loved, so I beg to differ on his viewpoint of my actions of being a wife. If I was so selfish, not supportive, or disrespectful. I would not have been helping when money was funny, nor would I have been by his side through sickness and health. He never went hungry. He always entered a clean home (even when his grown children didn't clean up behind themselves). It wasn't my daughter is my daughter only, and your children were your children only-they were ours. I wonder how all our kids got to college. Who helped them along the way (at least from our household)? Are you saying I had no parts of that? I did everything I could to make our family - a family.

No, I'm not perfect, and I know my vocabulary can be a little harsh. Still, the language I spoke and the tough love I had given was given to everyone. Yet, it wasn't enough. I was there for every function, doctor appointment, and everything you had to do; I worked behind the scenes to ensure all went well and was well. Yet, it wasn't enough. I began to feel unappreciated. I began to feel used and misunderstood. I began to feel disrespected and unsupported.

Most importantly, I felt the love was gone, and that's enough for me to take a step back and reevaluate my life. Separation was to occur so that restoration could happen, but only finding out working it out was not an option. So, I question, did you ever really love me? Or did you love what I could do for you?

Even though I felt this way, I still wanted my marriage, but is there hope since I was six months out of the house? I refused to go back to the way things were, and you refused to see that our marriage was in danger. Every time I spoke to you, I always ended up being the villain because I was the one who packed and left. I had to make a drastic change to open your eyes, but now I wonder if you ever wanted them to be open in the first place? Questions I have asked and yet have received an answer. So, I continued to pray to God, asking what I shall do?

> *Forget the former things; do not dwell on the past. See, I am doing a new thing! ... ~Isaiah 43:18 (NIV)*

Throughout this whole ordeal from day one of this journey, God has been doing a new thing. Something new in me, my mind, my body, my heart, and my soul. I am not the same person I was – not even six months ago. I can look in the mirror and be at peace with myself most of the time. Most days are better than others, but the reality remains the same, I will not go back to the way things used to be in my life. I will not go back and forth another day with the "What ifs" and the "Could ofs." I will not spend another day toiling in my mind the possibility of what could have been if there is no effort on your part to reconcile.

Lord knows I love the man I married, and my heartstrings are tightly attached. Still, I can't feel unwanted, unloved, and unappreciated another day. Then there is the will of my Father – I want to ultimately do His will and not mine, even if it is the desire of my heart.

I've witnessed throughout my whole life, even when I was in the world, those who commune with You, build a relationship with You, and live for You get the desires of their hearts. It may not be when they think, but Your promises have never returned void. I've never seen the righteous forsaken. So, I guess the real question is, what does the desire of my heart look like?

Talking to the Boss:

Abba Father,

You have told me repeatedly that I am worthy, I am royalty, and I am chosen. I don't need to bargain with anyone about who I am and whose I am. I'm thankful for the constant reminders that I need to live out my God-Given Identity. No one could love me better than You or me, so why should I settle for mediocre.

You have given me a word about integrity. In bargaining with someone about your life, somewhere along the line, you can lose your integrity. I believe Erich Fromm said it best,

> **"Integrity simply means not violating one's own identity."**

I will not violate my identity in You, Jesus. I know where my help comes from. I know that when I face trials and tribulations, You will be the one that saves me from it all. You deserve the glory and the honor, just because You are the Great I Am. You declared in your word that **"You will rescue the godly from the trials..."** (2 Peter 2:9, NIV), and this I would hold true until I take my last breath. I will not allow others to belittle me, take advantage of me, disrespect me, and take on their definition of who I am. I stand on who I am destined to be.

> **"You are a chosen people, a royal priesthood, a holy nation, God's special possession...."**
> **~1 Peter 2:9 (NIV)**

Who could not rejoice on those words alone? No matter what anyone says, I am chosen. I was created in His image, which announces how much He loves me. For that matter, He loves all of us who believe in Him, who lifts Him up and magnifies His name. There is nothing that can separate me from the Love of God. This is enough for me to hold on to, even in my darkest hours and my worst days.

"Christ gives me the strength to face anything."
~Philippians 4:13 (CEV)

Even the naysayers, the backbiters, the gossipers, or anyone who doesn't want me to soar high in You, Jesus, will stop me from walking in my God-Given Identity.

I will not bargain with another soul again, In Jesus Name.
I know who I am… The Daughter of a King.

Bargain with Who?

You say I'm not worthy.
You say I'm a disgrace.
You say I'm hideous, even in the face.
You say my Spirit is mean.
And my heart is cold,
You say my life you will always control.

Will I bargain with you another day?
Words you speak to me which cause dismay.
I'm tired of your wicked, low-down dirty blues.
I believe it's time to buy myself a new pair of shoes,
So, I can walk away from the words so untrue,
I will not stay another day and bargain with you!

Bargain with who? Not you!
Tired of the tears you have put me through.
How much more understanding could I be?
With the selfish "me's" and the manipulative ways
The many lies and deceit,
Yes, it's time for me to flee.
Getaway to a place where I can just be,
Be free to love how God showed me,
Tired of the pleas and cries for help,
Pain in my heart every time I yelp.

Will I bargain with you another day?
Words you speak to me which cause dismay.
I'm tired of your wicked, low-down dirty blues,
I've finally bought those new pair of shoes,
Because I'm walking out on you,
Away from the words I deemed as untrue.
Nope, I won't stay another minute, hour, or day--

Bargaining with you...

I will never forget you

In Spite of Me, being me and me getting in the way of my destiny,
You, my Father, have never forgotten about me.
You have never given up on me and the promises you made to me.
You loved me, even when I didn't love myself.
Many have failed me and proven to be unloyal, but not you,
You stood there with me and endured.

Then, one day I heard you say, my daughter,

In the shadows, I saw your doom, but thanks to my glorious light,
Your flower will finally bloom.
There is nothing more fabulous in the world,
then to receive the love back from my favorite girl.

Always remember your life is in my hands,
And I know each and every plan.
You can't alter the design,
Even though your choices will allow you to try.
Trust is all I need, and when you do,
I will make a believer out of you.
No matter what, my promises will remain faithful,
and another thing, I will always love you.

The door is open, will you receive the love, joy, and peace,
I have granted thee.
Shadows may linger on the path I have for you,
but my light will shine brightly,
So, you can see your way through.

Despite you, being you and getting in the way of your destiny.
I am Your Father, who will always love his baby.
The best thing about my love is that it conquers
and rules above all.

        So, you see, my beautiful daughter,
       I could never forget who you are to me.

Prayer

Father God, I thank you this day for being a patient and understanding Father. You have shown your daughter love, grace, and kindness through all my hurt, pain, heartaches, and headaches. You have held me even during my temper tantrum state. You waited patiently for me to realize you are right there going through my feelings with me, just as I was going through them. I shall continue to exalt Your name and give You all the honor and praises. You have taught me to embrace Your gentleness while You showed uninterrupted support. You've reminded me how much I'm loved despite what I might see through my natural eyes or what I might hear through my natural ears.

Father, Thank you for Your daily words of edification. Words to draw me closer to where I should be and eliminate the waste that hinders my relationship with You. Words that infuse your strength into me daily. Words that can encourage me no matter the state I am in. Words that establish the faith you desire for me to have. Words that remind me never to seek revenge but leave vengeance to You. The words which speak of me being a fool in Your eyes if I remain stricken with anger and judgment instead of forgiving those who have done me wrong.

Oh Lord, You are extraordinary. Thank you, Father, for reminding me to keep malice, wrath, anger, and bitterness as far away from my heart as possible. So, my mouth won't pour out the issues of my heart.

Today, I declare peace over my mind—the peace of the Lord within my heart. There is no weapon the enemy can form against me that will prosper. The enemy will never win my heart, mind, or soul, for the Spirit of the Lord dwells within me, and all His riches and glory will shine above all.

I declare hell has no fury, and no demon can withstand the majestic power of the Lord, Jesus Christ. He is the ruler of ALL THINGS.

I declare this day,
>Peace surrounds me,
>Joy surrounds me,
>Love surrounds me,
>All the days of my life.

In Jesus Name,
Amen!

Dying

Temptation comes from our own desires, which entices us and drag us away. These desires give birth to sinful actions. And when sin is allowed to grow, it gives birth to death.

James 1:14-15 (NLT)

Dying:
1. *Approaching death*
2. *Gradually ceasing to be*
   (Merriam-Webster.com)

What is spiritual death?
To have our souls alienated or separated from God because of the act of sin. God, who is our source of life and light, will turn His face from sin. A spiritually dead person only looks to appease himself. What profits a man to gain the whole world and lose his own soul? (Matthew 16:26).

Remember, when you are being tempted, do not say, "God is tempting me!" Scripture says God will never tempt His children to do wrong. Temptation comes from you and your fleshly desires. Your temptation will entice and captivate you, charming you away from the loving and compassionate hands of Our Father. When you allow your passion and temptations to fester and grow roots and leaves, you are causing yourself to sin most sinfully. Appeasing the flesh draws you nearer to death… a death that can be so horrific, an end where there is no joy, peace, or light. A death that allows you to walk the earth with no sight, no vision-just darkness… My God, I'm dying. I don't want to die.

During my moments of anguish, frustrations, and loneliness, the enemy used this opportunity-an open door- to attack, attack my very soul. The enemy played on my emotions-his chance to attract and beckon me to the very worst part of me… my flesh.

The first time I slept with someone, Oh my! It felt soo good. I was engulfed in his arms, and once again, I felt sexy, not loved, but sexy. Then, something happened I never expected; I got convicted. I got convicted so bad; I thought I could never look at another man again. It had been three months, and I didn't even want to stand next to a man. My heart pounded every time I stood next to eye candy. Oh, My Gosh! I didn't want my pheromones to attract another man in life... LOL! (Laughing out Loud). I know the opportunity would come when I would love again, but I wanted to stand clear for now.

Just when I let my guard down and thought I was "safe." Things were going well in my life; I felt I recognized the enemy and began calling him out before he attacked. Indeed, I was wrong. The distractions from work and doing things started to come in from the left and right, and then the tempter knocked at my door. I came off the wall to take a breath, and I was ambushed. The tempter came once again, and this time it was in the form of a handsome young, calm, cool, and collected black male. He had arms like Hercules and abs like a washboard. He was tall and sleek, and just looking at him, you knew he tasted like your favorite chocolate bar... *Oh My! What would I do to get a taste of that?* I thought.

I asked a question, and who would have known I would soon find out. My thoughts would quickly become a reality. With the anger and bitterness from my separation, now festering up in my heart more and more, that was the fire the enemy needed, and I was right where he wanted me... Off the wall with my boxing gloves off, the enemy had me cornered. My final thought was, *"Who could resist their favorite chocolate bar when you are really hungry? Not I..."*

Just like that, I was thinking only about myself and disregarded the voice of God. He spoke and spoke and spoke, and I ignored Him.

One day while cleaning my house, I heard Him say, *"What little faith do you have, my daughter? Haven't I been a good provider? Have I not shown how powerful, loving, and merciful I am? Didn't I hold your heart in my hands to stop it from continuously breaking into tiny pieces? Haven't I hidden you from your enemies? I have called you my friend, and this is how you treat me. What loyalty do you have to me? What little faith do you have, my daughter?"* Suddenly, a cloud of self-destruction rested over me. I was killing myself, and there was nothing anyone could do about it. I was blinded by hurt, frustration, anger, and bitterness that I could no longer see. Oh! How the tempter had his claws in me. He was young and built. I am thick, plump, and juicy. When he lifted this plus-sized woman and caressed me from one room to the next, he was in there like swimwear.

The first night with the tempter was gentle and sweet. The tempter was a complete gentleman, opened the door for me, and helped me up in his truck. We had a good conversation, and sex was nowhere on the menu. He had goals and ambition; he was in his mid-thirties and had no children. The first thing I thought when he said that was, *"I didn't have to fight with no one else, disrespectful child."* Ohhhh No! I was wrong for thinking that. I immediately threw that thought out of my mind. I had better things to think about, like this whole meal that was sitting across from me. Dinner was excellent, and I didn't have to cook—a gourmet meal right out of the tempter's kitchen. The presentation was on point, and at the end of the night, I was returned to my humble abode with only his sweet, soft lips to remind me of him until next time.

Random morning messages of encouragement, hope, and conversations of better days flooded my world for a whole month. Oh yeah, the heat was beginning to turn up, and I was all the way distracted. I was in the line of fire and had no idea I was about to get burned. Our subsequent encounter was just as eventful and sweet, and he was still a gentleman. After dinner, it was movie time, but the movie ended up watching us. His hands began to serenade my body, and his lips began to explore the creases and crevices of my neck. His mouth was so soft, and his hands were so gentle that I didn't want it to end. Then it happened, his phone rang. He ignored it, but I couldn't help to think it was a warning for me. Should I stop? The phone rang again. I asked him, "Shouldn't you get that-whoever it is, they really want to talk to you?" When I sit back and think, *it was my warning; it was a call for me to go home. My Father was telling me to get it moving, or else I would be in big trouble.* Like the rebellious child, I ignored my Father and lost all control in the tempter.

I was subjected to the tempter. With every breath, I was engulfed in the sin of lust and fornication. His mouth explored parts of my body; I didn't remember what it felt like until that moment. From the nape of my neck to the tip of my toe was fair game for the tempter. I indulged in the moment of bliss. Every stroke and every kiss were slow and gentle. This went on for hours, no way could I let it stop, but even I had to get ready for work in the morning. How would I make it through the day, but guess what, I didn't care? I was on another planet and couldn't read any relevant signals if I needed to. I was in trouble and headed for disaster. My God, I was slowly dying.

God had turned his face. He would not dare look at my sinful self, not another second, minute, or hour. I indulged in the fantasy, but trust me, it was not without consequence. My prayer life was suffering. The anger and bitterness from my separation rose to the forefront of my heart. I began to recollect moments of discord in my relationship with my husband. I began to reminisce on our most precious moments and fumed at that thought of him not fighting for it just as I was. I was spiraling out of control, losing focus on my priorities. Instead of stopping and pressing the reset button, I decided to run the derailed train into another train on the track, killing myself and maybe even those attached to me.

I had a dream that made me stop and think for a second. After the first dream of zombies, I realized God stopped talking to me. I knew He was there, I felt His presence, but He was silent... or was He? I got mad, and that was the best thing and the worst thing I could have done. It was the best thing because it made me stop. It was the worst thing because anger was in my heart for God. After all, He had done for me, I got mad at God for my life. Wait a minute; I got angry at God for the poor choices I was making. What was I thinking? With the dream of zombies, I knew God was speaking, but I wasn't listening.

I began to pull back from the tempter. Fewer conversations, fewer visits- the battle really began. He wanted to spend more time with me, and I was in a place of contemplation. I tried to appease my flesh, and doing so would cause me to die.

But the mercy of God reigned over me. A series of dreams and a word of correction changed my life at that moment.

Dream 1:
I was driving a car and drove it straight into the lake. I was drowning, and there was no one to save me.

Dream 2:
I was walking in the streets of my hometown. All around me were drug dealers, prostitutes, gang members. Every aspect of life I've ever experienced was surrounding me. The crazy part was they were all blind. They had no eyes, and they could not see, but they walked and talked as if nothing were wrong with them as if they could see. I woke up pleading for God's mercy that morning. I knew I was dying, and the dream was so realistic, I thought I was already dead.

Immediately, I erased every number in my phone who were distractions, rejectors, users, abusers, or anyone who meant me no good. I did a clean sweep and deleted them from all avenues of connection. I was sure about one thing; I didn't want to die.

Dream 3:
I was sitting by a tree crying. There was no evidence of why I was weeping crocodile tears, but I was. Suddenly, the root of the tree had begun to rise from the ground. It was now exposed. I woke up once again pleading God's mercy over my life. That morning, I began to wonder was it too late. Have I killed the only chance of hope, peace, or joy in my life? I prayed that morning that my Father didn't turn His face from me. If so, I was doomed.

But surprisingly, a word of correction came forth so sharp it cut like a freshly sharpened machete was going through my heart. The women God surrounded me with prayed and interceded over my life-pleading His mercy. They pleaded and cried out to the Lord for another chance. I begged God not to turn His back on His daughter. Instead, He says,

"For when you live by the flesh, you are about to die. But if the life of the Spirit puts to death the corrupt ways of the flesh, we then taste His abundant life."
~Romans 8:13 (TPT)

"If you are guided by the Spirit, you won't obey your selfish desires.
~Galatians 5:16 (CEV)

"Put to death all that is fleshly of you. I've already been crucified once; how many times are you going to crucify me? You are to carry your cross and kill the works of your flesh daily. You are to live according to the Spirit and put to death the deeds of your body so that you may have eternal life. I shall bless you with limitless qualities no man could ever give you. I will bless you with qualities of:
Joy that overflows.
Patience that endures.
Kindness in action.

A life full of virtue.
Faith that prevails.
Gentleness of the heart; *and*
Strength of the Spirit (Galatians 5:22-23, CEV).

"I love you, my child. I love you so much; I am always willing to save you. I needed your attention, and fortunately, I know how to get it. I know you love me, but the truth of the matter is, I don't realize how much you love me, and until you figure that part out, the tempter will always try to sneak in. I have the power to do all things, but I have given you dominion over the things of the earth, and that includes the enemy. Feast on that for a while-allow that to minister to your spirit-you can tell the mountain to move, and it shall move. So, this day forth, I want you to throw off your sinful nature and your former way of life, which is corrupted by lust and deception. Instead, let the Spirit renew your thoughts and attitudes. Put on your new nature, created to be like God-truly righteous and holy." (Ephesians 4:22-24, NLT)

I have not reached the end of God's mercy, love, or kindness.
Thank you, Father, for giving me a second chance.

Talking to the Boss:

Abba Father,

Oh My! What was I thinking? I just wasn't, and it almost cost me my life. Yet again, Father, You have shown how much You love a little wrenched like me. You snatched me out of the enemy's hands, and You have declared I am your child. You said, **"You are no longer a servant; you are my friend"** (John 15:15). You have told me, **"You have given me power, love, and self-control, and not the spirit of fear"** (2 Timothy 1:7). Fear is a trick of the enemy. There is nothing I should ever be afraid of. If I fear anyone, it should be a fear (reverence) of You, Jesus. There is no other name greater than your name, and in the middle of you snatching me out of a dying state, I realize that.

> *"So do not fear, for I am with you; do not be dismayed, for I am your God. I will strengthen you and help you; I will uphold you with my righteous right hand."*
> *~Isaiah 41:10 (NIV)*

I was on the verge of allowing the enemy to steal me away from this glorious promise from the Lord. The covenant he has made with me to be fearless in all that I do. I almost lost that.

> *"And we know that God causes everything to work together for the good of those who love God and are called according to his purpose for them. For God knew his people in advance, and he chose them to become like His Son...."*
> *~Romans 8:28 (NLT)*

In the beginning, I thought of my near-death experience as a failure. But during my prayer of repentance and tears of sorrow, You quickly reminded me, You are a forgiving and merciful God. You love me so much that mercy has surrounded me. Your love is sufficient to heal all things. Oh, My God! Thank you for the reminder; no one could condemn me, not even me. My Father has forgiven me, and my Savior has interceded on my behalf (along with His obedient women servants). He reminded me of the adulterer woman when Jesus told her to go and sin no more. Those were His words to me this day, and for this, my heart rejoices. *"Go, daughter and sin no more."* I almost died, but God loves me so much, *"He has given His only Son as a sacrifice, so I should not, and will not perish but have eternal life"* (John 3:16). Thank you, Father, for granting me another chance to live.

Near-Death

I almost died trying to appease my flesh,
Believing I was living new and refreshed.
Chasing after all the world's treasures,
Only to hit a wall and many of life's displeasures.

I almost died trying to run away,
When all God wanted was for me to stay.
Stand and declare the warrior in me,
As He healed and delivered and set me free.

What was I thinking? I don't think I was.
Living in the claws and clenches of the prince of the world,
But only to find out, he had no declaration over God's little girl.
Father, you snatched me out of the enemy's hands,
Before he implemented his devious plans,
To allow me to die in my sinful way,
Paying my debt to him and living in doomsday.
Father, you snatched me out of the enemy's hands,
Before he was able to place another demand,
Over my life and that of my family,
And before he caused any calamity.
Father, you love me, this I see,
Yet again, You chose to save me.

If allowing Your Son to die wasn't enough,
I crucified Him further with all my bluff.
By not believing in who You called me to be,
I gave the enemy the opportunity to play with my destiny.

I almost died trying to satisfy me,
But I thank God He was able to see,
I'm worthy to be saved and set free,
Which started with a plea down on bended knee.

I almost died,
But now I live.
My flesh will be shattered and laid under my feet,
As I lift up my God, the one who really loves me.

Now I see the flesh shall die,
So, I can live off of God's eternal life's supply.

                    Thank God I will survive!!

My revelation:

My mind wants to do what is right by God's law because of the sin within me; I am a slave to sin. Jesus Christ is the answer to this problem. Jesus, You are the answer to the war between the spirit and flesh.

We must trust God wholeheartedly. His omniscience, sovereignty, faithfulness, His Omnipresence, His healing power, His mercy, and grace, but most importantly, His Love are reasons for us to trust God. He is the only one that can save us from ourselves. Daily, we fight spirits of principalities - we should never fight battles in the flesh - we could never be strong enough to fight any battle. Our flesh is the conduit to sin, and Jesus is the conduit to life. We had already lost the war when we believed we could fight a battle carnally. The enemy has eaten us alive, and now we are on the battlefield bleeding to death. Who wants to die like that?

Trust God in the war…
He is the only reason we will survive!

Note to Reader:

As you read this prayer, believe in your heart that Jesus died and rose in three days with all power in His hands. He has defeated the enemy, so He can set the captives free. We are those captives. God knew from the day we were born; we would be slaves to sin. ***But God!*** With all His love, kindness, mercy, and grace, He gave His Son, Jesus, to be that sacrifice. Don't be afraid to face the woman in the mirror. Through all her tears, faults, and shame, she, too, can be redeemed, repositioned, renewed, and respected, In Jesus Name.

> *"For the sinful nature is always hostile to God. It never did obey God's laws, and it never will."*
> *~Romans 8:7 (NLT)*

> *"This includes you were once far away from God. You were His enemies, separated from Him by your evil thoughts and actions. Yet now, He has reconciled you to Himself through the death of Christ in His physical body. As a result, He has brought you into His own presence, and you are holy and blameless as you stand before Him without a single fault."*
> *~Colossians 1:21-22 (NLT)*

> *"And I know that nothing good lives in me, that is, in my sinful nature. I want to do what is right, but I can't. I want to do what is good, but I don't. I don't want to do what is wrong, but I do it anyway. But if I do what I don't want to do. I am not really the one doing wrong; it is sin living in me that does it.*
> *~Romans 7:18 (NLT)*

Deliverance Prayer

Father God, Oh Mighty God,

I come to you this day with a heart of repentance. Thank you, Father, for your unconditional love. I believe, Father, you have given us Your only Son, Jesus Christ, to be our pure sacrifice. I believe in my heart, Jesus was beaten and bruised for my iniquities. Jesus rose on the third day with all power in His hands. Jesus, I thank you for redeeming me with Your blood, and now I belong to You, Jesus, and I want to live for you.

This day, I confess all my sins to You -known and unknown- I'm sorry for all the strife I have caused against You. I renounce all activities of sin this day. I forgive all those who have caused me harm, just as I want you to forgive all my sins. Jesus, I'm asking for forgiveness, and I desire to be cleansed with the precious blood that you have so freely sacrificed. Thank you for your blood, Jesus, that cleansed me of all my sins, and please make me white as snow. I bow before you, my deliverer, Jesus, asking for you to heal me and set me free. You know all my needs-You know every spirit that tried to bind me, torment me, or hold me hostage from my mother's womb. I stand on the promise, *"whoever calls you by name, Jesus, shall be delivered."* I stand on your promise, *"No weapon formed against me shall prosper."* I'm calling on you, Jesus, right now to hide me with your blood from any and every demonic spirit trying to attack me.

In the name of Jesus, I cast out the spirit of rebellion, the spirit of bitterness, the spirit of anger, the spirit of strife, the spirit of rejection, the spirit of loneliness, the spirit of insecurities, the spirit of depression, the spirit of paranoia, the spirit of confusion, the spirit of doubt, the spirit of deception, the spirit of manipulation, the spirit of self-deception, the spirit of cursing, the spirit of witchcraft, and the spirit of sexual impurity, I send you all back to the pits of hell where you came from, In Jesus Name. Jesus, deliver me and set me free. Satan, I renounce you and all your trickery. I release myself from your strong man, never to return to my house again, In Jesus Name. I command you to leave me right now, In the Mighty Name of Jesus.

Amen!
Amen!
Amen!

Guilt

> My dear children, I write this to you so that you will not sin. But if anybody does sin, we have an advocate with the Father-Jesus Christ, the Righteous One. He is the atoning sacrifice for our sins...
>
> 1 John 2:1-2 (NIV)

Guilt:
A feeling of deserving blame for offenses.
(Merriam-Webster Dictionary)

> *Guilt is aversive and like-shame, embarrassment, or pride- has been described as a self-conscious emotion involving reflection on oneself.*
>
> *(Psychology.com)*

What do you have to feel guilty for? I never want to feel guilty for anything I do, so I pondered on the reasons why I left during this most challenging rollercoaster of emotions. I never wanted to regret my decisions, and even though for a little while, I did feel guilty. That phase of emotions was quickly eradicated when you decided to manipulate the guilt I was feeling.

Guilt can sometimes come upon someone for various reasons. It could be an act that was committed or thought; in my case, the action was I left you... Was it the right choice? Was I making the right decision? Was I obedient to the dreams and the warnings and the clear voice to separate? The voice resonated so clearly in my spirit, so it had to be You, Jesus. Just holding onto those words brought me comfort, and guilt couldn't last in my house. Another reason guilt will fall upon someone is when they believe they failed; failed to complete a task or duty. In my case, I thought I failed at my marriage. I made a vow before God, so how come I felt like I was the only one that honored it. But here I am, feeling guilty. Then, I began to feel guilty because of the immoral thoughts I was having. The ungodly thoughts were running rapidly in my mind; I felt like the enemy played basketball there. Quickly, I had to be reminded that *I am a new creature in Christ, and He has renewed my mind. Every thought had to be taken captive by the Word of God.* Therefore, I've asked why I should feel guilty... We both played a part in the role of my leaving. I was not going to spend another day blaming myself.

The anger and bitterness started to subside. I was filling myself with the word, and the people God surrounded me with were PUSHinG me into another place in Jesus. We must never forget we are not perfect. We will make mistakes, but God is such a merciful Father; if you allow Him, He will always be there to assist you in getting it right. God is Omniscient. Doesn't it feel good to know someone in your corner, knows the truth, knows your struggles and thoughts, and doesn't hold you hostage? God embraces you with His Love and Kindness. That's what He did during this quirky rollercoaster ride of emotions. So, what do I have to feel guilty for?

I couldn't believe that I felt some type of way to save myself from any more heartache; that doesn't even make sense. It hit me. The realization hit me when I felt guilty and going through the most annoying rollercoaster ride of emotions; here comes "the love of my life," laying it on thick. He was trying to make me feel guilty for leaving. Yes, I know I packed it up and left, but I didn't need you to remind me of it every time we spoke sarcastically. As if I'm not already having a hard enough time accepting the fact, I was obedient, even though I'm grateful. I was obedient to the voice of God, and it hurt. It hurt like hell. Sometimes obedience causes us to feel hurt and pain, not in a wrong way, but it is a release. I was releasing the things that cause pain and hurt to keep you there. **When we are hurting while being obedient to God, we must remember that our will is dying and making room for God's will in our lives.**

I think when we beat ourselves up for making drastic and dramatic choices, the enemy has us right where he wants us. But when, and I mean when, we get that inkling of strength and realize you are being manipulated in the process, you muster up the remainder of that strength to fight.

I had a desire to prove to myself I could make it.
In doing so, I had to do some things along the way.

1. **I had to forgive myself.**
    I had to stop replaying every horrible thing that had happened to me in my mind. I was beginning to subject myself to a life of torment. Paul Boese said it best, *"Forgiveness does not change your past, but it enlarges your future."* Forgiving myself was for me and not for the abuser, user, or manipulator. It was so I could walk into my freedom and my purpose.

> *"You intended to harm me, but God intended it all for good. He brought me to this position so I could save the lives of many people."*
> *~Genesis 50:20 (NLT)*

2. **I had to realize that feeling guilty doesn't change a thing.**
   Who was I fooling? If I didn't understand the serenity prayer before, I sure do understand it now: *"Father, grant me the SERENITY to accept the things I can't change, the COURAGE to change the things I can, and the WISDOM to know the difference."* This prayer took on a whole new meaning for me. I'm not sure if it was because of the trials I was facing, but there are some things I must accept I can't change. The only thing I could change was me and how I handled it all.

3. **I had to revisit my values.**
   I was worth more than I was giving myself credit for. Once I realized I had no reason to feel guilty, I embraced forgiveness. In embracing forgiveness, I unlocked my truth. In unlocking my truth, I revealed I had true strength. I was unique, worthy, and had integrity. So, you see, I was worth more than I was giving myself credit for. I am loved... I was created in His image, He knew every hair that rested on my head, and I'm worth more than many sparrows. So, I am loved.

> *"Are not fives sparrows sold for two pennies? Yet, not one of them is forgotten by God. Indeed, the very hairs on your head are numbered, don't be afraid; you are worth more than many sparrows.*
> *~Luke 12:6-7 (NIV)*

4. **I had to take a step.**
   One step was all God was asking for. Trusting someone may seem to be an arduous task when your heart has been broken.

Trusting someone may seem even more strenuous when you have always felt like it won't get done right when you don't do it. Trusting someone can come with a cost - whether good or bad - and with my many experiences of poor choices in trust, it became a battle for me even to TRUST GOD... But God! He had planted many seeds through His faithful sowers, and I allowed Him to water the seeds to harvest.

"For I know the plans I have for you," declares the Lord, "plans to prosper you and not to harm you, plans to give you hope and a future."
~Jeremiah 29:11 (NIV)

"Delight yourself also in the Lord, and He will give you the desires and secret petitions of your heart. Commit your way to the Lord [roll and repose each care of your load on Him]; trust (lean on, rely on, and be confident) also in Him, and He will bring it to pass."
~Psalms 37:4-6 (AMPC)

Many have stated guilt is a normal reaction. It is an expected emotion for an individual who has a conscience. So, though this emotion for me has been short-lived, it was expected. I felt I didn't fulfill my promise to God and my spouse. I believed in my "couple of forever's," my fairy tale love story. The only thing was my fairy tale love story, which I now understand I didn't own because my life is not my own, to begin with. I was bought with a price, so my body is a temple that can no longer mingle with the likes (foolishness) of the world. Only God can take the folly of the world to conform to the wise. I will always love the man I married, but I could no longer mix with the negativity; peace and joy surround me. I understand trouble will still come my way. Still, I will respond to it positively, fighting my battles on my knees and not with my education or knowledge, but with the knowledge and wisdom of God. I understand my value, and I'm worth fighting for.

Talking to the Boss:

Thank you, Father, for not condemning me but saving me in my place of guilt (John 3:17). Today, I am reminded I am a sinner. I admit that aloud because the enemy will no longer hold me in that place of bondage. I am nothing without You, Jesus; it is Your blood that You have shed for me, that is keeping me today, and I thank you.

Father, You have been a provider through all this earthly mess. Knowing you are not a God of confusion, I trust You will continue to give me clarity as I walk closer to You. Father, I am allowing You to continue to rewrite my story, and I will not feel guilty for this.

Hebrews 8:12, *"For I will forgive their wickedness and remember their sins no more."* Father, if I've done or spoken contrary to Your will, please forgive me. If I was out of order during this transition in my life, please forgive me. But Father, I will no longer feel guilty another day for being obedient to the voice of You, Lord. You are my saving grace.

Surrounded by the darkness of the world,
Something so great stands out...
The love that you have for me,
The joy you desire to give me,
The peace that you rest upon me,
The faith to believe it all It's intentional.

To see life's trials and obstacles
Tremble at the sound of your name.
To meditate on the words you gave,
knowing every knee will bow in your grace.
Feeling confident, I will not grow weary and lose my heart.
It's intentional, and I know it from the start.

Surrounded by the darkness of the world,
But you died to save every woman and man, and every boy and girl.
The unnecessary weight shall be stripped away,
And tomorrow always brings forth a new and refreshed day.
The author and perfecter of my story,
You will forever receive my ultimate praise and glory.
It's the most fantastic feeling to know-
The love that you have for me,
The joy you desire to give me,
The peace that rests upon me,
You've given me the faith to believe it all.
Lord, You are intentional.

SHE IS...

She touches your very being and the remnants of your soul.
She has devised a plan that if you trust her,
you will be made whole.
She drives away pride and all your persevered speech,
She calls you to worship the very ground she walks,
And hearken to the words that only she speaks.
She desires you to fear the God that created her every being,
For He is the reason that she stands with grace, fearlessness,
and authority.
She offers you great success when you find her and embrace her.
She is designed to give you insight into His wise plan
that only He knows for your life.
      She is a keeper - a superwoman.
      She is understanding - a provider.
    She is courageous and strong - a fearless warrior.
     She draws you to the lover of your soul.
 She will love abundantly; just hold on to her unconditional love.
       She is faithful.
       She is glory.
    She is generous – she stands for love.

This mysterious woman imparts greater into those
whom she touches,
She multiplies everything that's in her clutches.
She increases the least of your belongings just to make you rich.
There is no lack in her, and she does it all without a hitch.

Trust Her,
Love Her,
Embrace Her too.
There is nothing but joy in the company of my boo.

She is the significant gain of confidence that you seek,
a wealth of income that is beyond your reach.
This abundant living that you speak so highly of,
comes from this remarkable woman named

WISDOM...

Prayer

Father God,

I come to you this day with a heart of repentance. Father, I ask that you forgive me for my sins that I have committed or thoughts that were not worthy of you knowingly or unknowingly. I ask you to cast my sins into the sea of forgetfulness. I'm thanking you, Father, for being a holy, loving, and merciful Father.

Humbled at your feet this day, I ask for forgiveness for allowing guilt to control my life. Thank you, Father, for hearing your daughter and removing guilt from the remnants of my soul, and wiping my slate clean with the Blood of Jesus. Thank you, Father, for reminding me to be kind and compassionate to others, forgiving them for their transgressions. Just as you have forgiven me, I'm welcomed into the beloved. Thank you, Father, for sending Your Son Jesus into the world not to condemn us but to save us. Therefore, who am I to judge, even myself. Through the Blood of Jesus, I'm redeemed and forgiven by the riches of His grace. Father, you are a merciful Father, and I thank you for reminding me to not walk according to my flesh but by the Spirit. I am fighting the spirit of principalities and not carnal battles. You have given me the power and authority to speak to mountains, and it shall be moved.

The spirit of guilt, you must go, In the Name of Jesus. You have no dwelling here. You have no dominion to torment me anymore. I'm sending you back to where you have been sent from.

Enemy, you are a liar and the father of lies. I will no longer believe anything you say. As I pray, guilt is leaving right now, In the Name of Jesus.

I am the daughter of the Most High God. And in Christ Jesus, I am a new creature, and since the old things have passed away, so you guilt shall die.

Father, fill me up with love, peace, forgiveness, joy, and all your characteristics in my vacant space. Fill me up with Your Word, the Word which restores and heals, In the Name of Jesus. I know my worth. I know who I am. I will walk, talk, and live as the daughter of the Sovereign God.

In Jesus Name,
Amen!

Depression

Come quickly, Lord, and answer me, for my depression deepens, don't turn away from me, or I will die. Let me hear of your unfailing love each morning, for I am trusting you. Show me where to walk for I give myself to you.

Psalms 143:7-8 (NLT)

Depression:
Feelings of severe despondency and dejection
(New Oxford American Dictionary)

Depression is a medical condition when genetics, hormones, nerve cell receptors, and brain functionality become abnormal.
(WebMD.com)

Many of life's most challenging obstacles can trigger depression. Depression does not discriminate; it doesn't matter what race, color, creed, ethnicity you are; once started, you must face a battle. Sometimes individuals don't even know it's coming; it can creep up on you and even be debilitating. But God! He has sent us a remedy to heal, deliver, and set the captives free, and His name is Jesus. Thank you, Jesus, for the Blood.

There were days when I didn't want to get out the bed; I didn't want to eat or even desired to shower (Thank God, I'm not a stink person). There were days I didn't want to speak to anyone; I felt they wouldn't understand. How could I get them to understand? I can't make him love me if he doesn't, no matter how much I wanted him to… And neither could they. If I couldn't get him to understand this trial was an enemy attack, and we were letting him win, neither could they. The enemy had one up on my husband and me because we couldn't unify and show love. The enemy's mission is to distort love so it can cause discord. The enemy hates to love: he can't live in love. He hates togetherness, and when we keep the blinders on our eyes; We won't see how to keep the enemy at bay, and that's to show love.

Love was the weapon to counterattack, it was the only way to save our marriage, and I was the only one fighting the battle. I lived long enough with him, believing our lives was just going to be how it was going to be. There was no room for change, not even within us. I was ready to face myself and some of the demons I carried, and sadly, he was unwilling to do so. I could no longer accept another person's abuse of words or abuse of attention to dictate my life.

Most importantly, I couldn't let another day go by where I didn't love the woman in the mirror. I was being held hostage in prison, the one I created and had planned to spend life in it. I gave myself a number and was willing to walk through life identified by that number (what others thought about me), and I couldn't do it anymore. I had to break free.

One of the things I'm indebted to is the emotional transitions I've experienced. It allowed me to face them, embrace them, and with Jesus walking me through them, it helped me realize that it's okay to have feelings.

"Then He broke through and transformed all my wailing into a whirling dance of ecstatic praise! He has torn the veil and lifted from me the sad heaviness of mourning."
~Psalms 30:11 (TPT)

"The Lord hears his people when they call to him for help. He rescues them from all their troubles. The Lord is close to the brokenhearted; He rescues those whose spirits are crushed."
~Psalms 34:17-18 (NLT)

"He will wipe all tears from their eyes, and there will be no more death, suffering, crying, or pain. These things of the past are gone forever."
~Revelations 21:4 (CEV)

I must admit God has blessed me with two magnificent spiritual mothers (not one, but two, I'm so lucky!) who have walked me through this process, along with my P.U.S.HinG sisters (My Red Cross Relief Team). Through the many words of encouragement, I was reminded of Joseph in the bible. Joseph was Jacob's son who was loved by his father but envied by his brothers. He had to go through an arduous path to get to his purpose. Joseph never gave up on God's promise, and that was prodigious of him. From the pit to the jail – he adhered to the affirmation of God. He lived with integrity and worked diligently even in his dark place, only to reach his purpose, which was Pharoah's palace. Joseph's story reminds me even in my dark place, I, too, shall hold on to the promises of God. That whatever the enemy *"uses to harm me, God intends to use it for His good to accomplish what is now being done, saving lives* (Genesis 50:20, NIV)." Joseph's purpose was to be in a position of power and authority to help his people (so are the purpose of us all, as disciples of Christ). Still, it did include some dark places, like rejection, being thrown in a pit, being sold into slavery, thrown in jail, amongst other things. Lastly, his position in the palace--Look at God! His words will never return unto Him void.

Some of us, like myself, would have given up a long time ago, believing God is not here anymore; He can't be by my side here. Quickly, I have learned that God is most robust in my feelings and many emotions in my dark place. He shows His love and strength even more; the critical question is, do we trust Him to be there amid it all? Joseph's story reminds me to persevere. Disregard the foolishness and all wickedness that is thrown at me. Who is more reliable, loving, and committed than our Father? Scripture says, *"We will walk through the valley of the shadow of death"* (Psalms 23), not stay in, live in, or rest in… notice He said **WALK THROUGH**. Scripture also says, *"The tongue has the power of life and death"* (Proverbs 21). We can either kill ourselves with the negativity or speak life to ourselves with positivity. In my depressive state, I had to break the silence and vocalize life to myself, and I was surrounded by women who did the same. I could no longer allow death words into my environment and atmosphere, even those thoughts in my mind. I had to let the Blood of Jesus captivate my thoughts and renew them. I had to allow Jesus into my heart, so He could mend the broken pieces and restore me. I had to let go and let God handle my issues and concerns, not some of them but all of them. Joseph taught me that I am stronger if God is on my side.

The enemy uses disorder and chaos to wreak havoc and destruction in our lives. He will use (if we are not careful) the thoughts of our minds and the issues of our hearts to successfully complete his mission (his mission to destroy humankind). During this period in my life, I learned it's imperative to silence the noise. Not monthly, nor weekly – but daily. Every day, silencing the noise around you with prayer, the reading of the word, sitting in that place of stillness while admiring God's masterpieces encompassing you allows you to listen to the following directives in His master plan, which He calls your life. Spending time talking with God and listening to Him will enable you to build your trust relationship and grant peace and serenity. This is the peace and tranquility, grace, and mercy that we don't deserve, but He freely gives to us. These are the characteristics of a magnificent Father. Knowing this makes anything I've ever been through worth it all.

I've also learned to decree some things because life and death lie in my mouth. It must flee when you confess for anxiety to leave since the Lord says we shouldn't be anxious for anything (Philippians 4:6). When you oust guilt and depression to another destination, can it no longer cause havoc in your life? No, it can't. Then, once you remove the mountains and walls which once blocked your path to greatness; fill up every vacant place with love, peace, joy, faithfulness, humbleness, gentleness, kindness, goodness, patience, and self-control, and watch how the sky turns blue - and going through valleys aren't so lonely anymore. You will develop an unprecedented strength so unexplainable and genuine love that's contagious. You will smile at times when you should be crying, and life becomes so much grander. When you walk through life knowing no matter how hard someone tries, you could never be knocked out unless you allow it. It's almost inevitable. You will feel like a superwoman… I sometimes do. With my newfound strength, If I fall, I can now get up, dust myself off, and armor up again because my Father will give directives on watching out for that same blow the next time. Thank you, Father, for being my Chief Cornerstone.

Killing me Softly, No More

Help me! I feel like I'm drowning.
A lot of the memories and pain still remain.
It's keeping me bound, filled with guilt and shame.
I stopped hearing the voice inside,
That once told me that my dream would be alive.
I let the enemy steal a piece of my soul,
And now, the ministry that was in me can't grow.
I let the gift of God die within me.
Lord, what have I done? What do you think of me?
Yet, another one of your children, Gone too Soon!
But the enemy thought he'd won,
He made me feel I was doomed.
Killing me softly; Inside, I cried. It left me so confused.
What? What am I to do?
Then came along the joy of merely YOU!

So, I begin to say Thank you!
Thank you for your love.
The joy and peace you've shared,
Loving me in those times when I thought no one cared.
You heard me; you listened to my heart cry,
You listened to my soul saying yes,
And from that day on, You were determined to give me rest.

I began to petition the heavens for healing, mercy, and grace,
And you spoke some words to me that helped sealed my fate.
Those words that were spoken to me,
Gave me life, and I would indeed embrace it.

"Blessed, you are my daughter, and your sins I have forgiven. Choose to walk with me, and I can give you a life worthy of living."

Heaven heard my cry, and my sins are now covered.
So, now I'll embrace the life that I've just discovered.
The old has passed away, and the new has risen.
I will no longer be a slave again and feel imprisoned.

Spread your wings and fly,
A new day is here!
No need to cry, my sister,
Victory is Here!

Acceptance

Lord, never forget the promises you've made to me, for they are my hope and confidence. In all of my affliction, I find great comfort in your promises, for they have kept me alive!
Psalms 119:49-50 (TPT)

I am alive.
I am accepted into the house of the beloved.
I am a survivor.
I am the Daughter of a King.

Talking to the Boss:

Thank you, Abba Father, for keeping me in a place of gratitude and servitude. As I begin to walk on my path towards my destiny, I know and understand that bitterness, anger, shame, and regret, amongst other feelings and emotions stemming from my divorce, cannot go with me.

Father, I thank you for the release and my cry out to you, Lord, because the love string that still was attached could only be cut and detached by You and You only. Thank you for reminding me, You are the author and finisher of my story, the beginning and the end, and every promise made to me is still mine. Your promises of being a provider, living abundantly, and being a waymaker have been kept by You, Father. Your commitments to bless me with a gift from my womb have been preserved. Your promise of You being a great deliverer has been kept. Yes, the promises that You have given me from my mother's womb *STILL* belong to me.

Lord, it is Your promises that had kept my head held high when I wanted to run and hide in shame. Your promises of who I am kept me from feeling guilty for walking away from a love I desperately wanted and could not save. Your promises of where you are taking me allowed me to release the spirits of bitterness, anger, hurt, and disappointment; they are not welcome where I am going. You reminded me that I couldn't make someone love me the way I felt I deserved, and I began to understand it wasn't like he didn't try, but he may not know-how. The saying, "Hurt people do hurt people," has proven itself correct in my case. My hurt has poisoned my husband, and his open wounds have been venomous to me. When I realized the weight of my pain and the hurt others have placed upon me, I was willing to go to the hospital of hope. I received my diagnosis, received my medicine of salvation and deliverance, and stayed in rehab to recover. Lord, I thank you for the midwives and nurses you have sent my way to keep me in my place of healing.

My God! You are an amazing Father for reminding me there are many things in life that I can't change. You have granted me the serenity to accept it; You reminded me of Your grace of strength and courage to change the things I can and then wisdom to know the difference. You desired me to believe and have faith in You. Jesus, I couldn't have made it without You loving me, protecting me, and guiding me.

You deemed me worthy; you opened your arms and welcomed me into the Kingdom of Royalty-A Daughter of a King. I've entered the House of the Beloved. You have given me the power and authority to speak those things as though they were. You reminded me that the rejection I felt wasn't against me but against the anointing, You placed on my life. Oh, My God! That word alone has freed me from the rejection of people. Hallelujah! I wasn't receiving the love and support from the one person I believed would love me no matter what- You quickly reminded me of my mistake. You said, "When a man finds a wife, He finds a good thing," but it wasn't him that was doing the finding, nor the chasing; it was me. Therefore, I wasn't found, and my faithful helpmate is still out there waiting--no looking--for me. One of the things I will remember now, my grandpa CG used to say, "Women are not hunters. They don't know how." It took me some time, but now I realize why he used to say that. Men are supposed to find their wives, not the other way around. God, now I can appreciate You even more when you say, You are preparing me to be that Proverbs 31 woman, and there are some pruning and purging that must take place. Once again, I must say, "Thank You."

On this day, I will hold on to the promises of love, abundant life, the favor of God, and man that rests over my life. I will hold on to the promises of peace and joy and walk with dignity, integrity, and faith like no other in this walk of life with You. I will step into the realm of the unknown with strength and courage. I will walk with a determination never to turn back to the way of "what was" I am embracing and becoming all that You have destined me to be.

In the face of adversity, I will trust You.
In the middle of the storms, I will trust You.
In the place of my grief, I will trust You.

I am a new creature in Christ.
The old (flesh) has passed away, and Na-Tasha will live again.

Thank you, Father, for the comfort of your love, on this day.

Breakthrough

Breakthrough!
Breakthrough the darkness I once called life.
Breakthrough the anger that cut like a knife.
Breakthrough the pain that once stole my heart away,
Breakthrough, God, I need your light today!

Breakthrough!
Breakthrough the fornication that once kept me bound,
Breakthrough the lies and deceit that pushed everyone around,
Breakthrough the rejection that kept me NOT feeling loved.
Breakthrough, God is welcoming me into the arms of the beloved.

As the clouds turn away into your marvelous light,
I see your love shining ever so bright.
You satisfy my heart by filling it with joy,
Joy is a piece of the puzzle that fills us up with love.

You see,
Without Joy – You cannot find peace.
Without Peace – You cannot find Righteousness.
Without Righteousness – You cannot find Humbleness.
Without Humbleness – You cannot find pure love.
Thank you for the breakthrough…

Breakthrough!
Breakthrough the darkness with your light,
Continue to let it shine ever so bright.
The joy of the Lord that fills you up all the days of your life,
Is His strength and courage to lift you to stand and fight!

Let go of the struggles.
Let go of the strains.
Let go of the things that aren't meant for you to change.
Pick up, Joy.
Pick up, Peace.
Pick up, Love that conquers and defeats all.
Breakthrough!

Your breakthrough is here.
It is at the doorstep of your heart.
Open up! Let Him in!
And Victory will rise until the very end…

                    Breakthrough!

Prayer

Lord, My Abba Father,

I'm resting in your bosom this day; it's such a safe and powerful place of refuge. In my time of grieving, you have given me the strength and courage to endure. As you wrap your arms around me, and in the midst, you're planting my feet on solid ground, I declare your words over my life; there is no fear in You. The storms may feel like they are raging and crashing, but You have eradicated me by speaking, "Peace Be Still," and the raging storm responded with stillness.

My Abba Father, the Lord of Everything; every tear that has fallen has been captured by You, only to be released in the good soil (my soul) that You have tilled within me. Continue to hold me, Father, and never let me go. Continue to keep me and comfort me in my time of grief.

I declare the blessings of Your Love to fall on me endlessly. I declare the enemy would not come into my life and flood it with confusion and chaos; I will recognize you, satan, and send you back to the pits of hell. My Father is ruler over you, and He will keep me covered through all things. Healing and restoration will take place in the mighty name of Jesus. These are the blessings of the Lord that I will declare over my life.

In Jesus Name.
Amen!

What Does Freedom Mean to Me?

Gasping for air, I suddenly can't breathe,
The enemy of lies has been resting on me.
Thoughts in my mind, I'm suddenly confused,
This burning aspiration for being the woman you so gracefully choose.
Flames are higher than I've ever seen before,
They're burning away my inflictions,
now all I can do is fall to the floor.

While on my knees, this light appeared,
While burning gracefully, you whispered in my ears,
"What does your freedom mean to you?"
I replied, with tears in my eyes, and all I've said was true…
It means to rid the pain of yesterday,
The abuse, the addictions, the lies I've betrayed.
It means drawing near to your glorious light,
And I would never give up without a fight.
It means living in the image you created me to be.
And remembering to be humble and live graciously.
It means peace and joy follows my world,
And best of all, I can help save my little girl.

Rewiring my mind to live again because the hardest part of living,
Is seeing without any vision.
The darkness is going, and I stand a new
Burning away the old to get closer to you.

The glorious light shined brighter than ever before.
Then appeared before me this bright open door.
"Come, my dear child, I shall never leave,
I'm running to you, just as you're running to me."
My heart melted, and I felt warm & fuzzy inside,
I've lived my life long enough in the darkness and the lies.
But the warmness of your voice reassured me that your love for me
is genuine, and it's meant just for me.

My paradigm has shifted, and all is well.
I have embraced your philosophy,
When you say my life is destined for greatness,
and my purpose is needed as your kingdom prevails.
The fire has subsided deep inside of me,
And I feel the pushing and pressing to destroy my next ideology.

You are my Father, and I am your child,
You will never leave me broken, not even for a while.
You have sacrificed your life for the love of me,
And indeed, I will embrace the freedom that you've paid for me.
No longer gasping for air,
Ohhhh! I can finally breathe.
I am the woman of God; you've called me to be.
I died gracefully. So, I can be free.

Now I understand what my freedom means to me.

Will I Ever Love Again?

    I just want to give up on love. I have made many poor choices in my life for the sake of love. The satisfaction of my flesh imposed my decisions. Even while living in the world, the struggle is real. I'm not going to deny it, but it felt sooooo good to be wrong, but it feels even better to live correctly and reap the rewards that are so much grandeur.

    When I got married, I just knew it was forever. We would grow old, play with our grandchildren, and enjoy this thing called life together. It wasn't until I got married, the heat really turned up on me. I had made the first step to living righteously by getting married. I no longer wanted to "shack up" with a man or merely sleep with a man with no protection from God himself. I started to believe the teachings I was receiving about God. He was beginning to become life to me. So, when the heat turned up, I began to pray more, and revelation started to happen. I began to look at the woman in the mirror. I began examining myself. *"Jesus, what are you doing?"* became a daily question out of my mouth.

    Even though I married for love, my marriage wasn't built on love. Christ wasn't the head of our lives, and when I made Him the head of my life and declared my house belongs to Christ – and began living it, the struggle became real.

> *"For our struggle is not against flesh and blood, but against the rulers, against the authorities, against the powers of this dark world, and against the spiritual forces of evil in the heavenly realms."*
> ~Ephesians 6:12, NIV

My fight was not carnal; it was spiritual. I quickly learned I stepped into something I wasn't quite prepared for.

Oh, My God! I was about to get the best hands-on training I've ever endured in life, and my teacher was the greatest of them all, God.

Trusting, believing, and living Christ-like takes a change of heart and mind. What do you do when the strongholds are welcomed into your home? You Pray! Some might say stay and fight, which I did for a long time. I never wanted to give up. Others would say leave and learn, so you focus on understanding how to fight and learning whatever tactical strategies you need to fight. After getting whooped a few times, I chose the latter.

Now that I'm gone, I can see clearly. It wasn't my husband who didn't love me; it was the strongholds that we carried collectively and welcomed into our home, simply trying to blind us. I was never supposed to see my worth, and neither was he. Even now, when I try to explain it was all a trick of the enemy, he still doesn't want to see or simply can't see. My husband didn't want to or couldn't face the man in the mirror to no fault of his own. That's when my fairy tale ride through life with my coach and horses turned into a pumpkin, and my grandeur horses turned into mice (Thanks NY, I'm scared of mice). I never wanted to change anyone in my house; I loved them just as they were, and I knew God would do the changing. But I wanted, needed, and deserved respect while going through my change. I was beginning to see my worth, and I was determined not to settle for anything less than that anymore, no matter who it came from. At the beginning of the revelations, I began to do what any good Christ-like wife would do. I prayed harder but was I being effective? I had so much to learn, but I never stopped praying; God, touch his heart and opens his eyes to Your life-changing words. God remove me out of the way and restore what the enemy has tried to steal. I know God is capable of doing anything. If He did it for me before, I know He can do it for anyone.

I told myself a thousand times that I would never love again, but when I said that, I was not consulting about love from the one I should have been waiting for to send it to me in the first place. It was God, who I should have looked upon to send me love – not Na-Tasha. Can I ever love again?

So, I have derived what a man should look like for me. I was reminded God knows the one I need to PUSH me into my destiny. He knows the one I need to walk beside me as I walk alongside Him. Thank you for the reminder, but you also said you would give me my heart desires (Psalms 37:4) if my way pleases You. So, I will "Write it down and make it plain" (Habakkuk 2:2). If this is Your will, Father, allow me to be introduced to a man that fits my heart's desires and let Your will be done in my life.

1. This man **MUST** love God. The word says Husbands love your wives, just as Christ loved the church (Ephesians 5:25). If he doesn't love God, can he undeniably love me with God's same love for his children? Man can falter and fail, but if he lives daily trying to kill flesh daily, we accomplish the same goal – To have a heart like God, showing genuine love.

2. This man **MUST** communicate. Communication is the key to a lasting relationship. I don't care if we disagree and you need to walk outside to get some air and calm down; before we go to bed, we should compromise. I never said you

wouldn't think I'm sickening or get on your everlasting nerve and vice versa, but we should find a median before going to bed. At least, we shouldn't allow many days to pass angry; that's a no-no. I believe this level of communication shows respect and our undeniable love for one another. Will this take time to master? Absolutely, but if we are willing to work it out, a greater love will be accomplished.

3. This man **SHOULD** be spontaneous. I'm a whimsical romantic. I love to walk on the beach and the park. I love impromptu signs of affection. Flowers or fruit baskets delivered to the job showing how much you appreciate me and the love we share. Maybe it might seem a little extreme, but it's the random acts of love that keep a girl wanting more. Don't get me wrong; it's not about the money; it's a reminder of how much you care.

4. This man **MUST** work hard but willing to play hard too. Bills will never go away. Managing multiple streams of income (speaking it into existence) will take a lot of hard work, but spending "US" time together is just as important. Going back to number 3, that's why those random acts of love are essential. We can get so caught up chasing a life that we can forget about the meaningful things in our lives.

5. This man **MUST** be family-oriented. I love family, and not just blood family, but my extended family too. Family functions are influential. It's a level of support and love I display towards the people I love, so he must be family-oriented.

6. This man **MUST** demonstrate love. God is love. Love for humanity, love for nature, love for life. Every day, we should strive to be Christ-like, not taken advantage of, but demonstrate how we are saved through love. Spreading the Good News of the love and hope we have, just as God has shown to us.

This man doesn't have to be a supermodel, even though that might not be so bad (just kidding!). He just needs to have a heart for Jesus. He may have struggles because, guess what, I have struggles too. He doesn't have to be perfect because, indeed, I'm not, but he must strive and fight to be Christ-like. We live in the flesh, so surely we will fall, but we must be willing to get up, dust ourselves off, and continue to work into our God-given purpose and destiny.

Every day, I strive to let go of my will to walk into God's perfect will for my life. Is he willing to do the same? Indeed, He must. So, I ask, Will I ever love again?

Even though I wanted to give up on love, I recognize I'm created to be loved. God created humanity to be loved by Him, to have a personal and intimate relationship with Him. He also felt it was not suitable for a man to be alone, thus creating a woman (Genesis 2:18). Therefore, who am I to deprive myself of God's promise to me; a man shall leave his mother and father to be one with his wife (Genesis 2:24). For this reason, I will allow myself to open my heart once again to love. This time, allowing God to dictate who walks into it, giving me discernment to His Spirit, so I'm willing to see and hear as He sees fit.

Can I ever love again?
Trusting and believing in God this time around will permit me to love again. He would have closed all doors of hurt, bitterness, pain, and discord; to fill me up with joy, peace, humility, and happiness. As He continues to take me on a journey, I would only be able to go on with Him. I will learn to love myself first. I will embrace being a King's kid; while developing the discernment necessary to choose, one is worthy to walk alongside me as I continue this journey with Christ. My Father says, "I WILL LOVE AGAIN."

I have had some unforgettable memories from my first love (my daughter's father) until my first husband. These memories will always be a part of me forever. I also have some heartaches, disappointments, and misunderstandings; both the joys and pains have been learning tools. Though, no two men are alike in any embodiment. I have one component to the equation now that I didn't have then, and that's Jesus. I can trust Jesus to loose and bind things that I need to let go of and things I need to persevere during this journey called life. I know I will face adversities along the way. You're mistaken if you think you won't ever be tested because you are a believer and follower of Christ. That's the enemy fooling you. We must be willing to carry our cross daily, declaring God's goodness, mercy, and love over our lives and the lives of others. The enemy hates when we demonstrate love. I must be willing to open my heart to my friends, as well as my enemies if I'm declaring to love as God loves. There is no way the enemy will reap havoc in my house by trying to trick me into believing I can't love or be loved. I will not stay lonely forever. When God reckons, my Boaz (a Godly man respectful, kind, compassionate spiritual, and a channel for happiness) will stroll into my life, ready, willing, and able to love me.

Will I ever love again? Yes, I will lift my head, take my grave clothes off and put on my most extravagant dress, throw on my best wig (I have hair, just hate doing it), put on my sexiest pumps (I love the way my legs look in heels), and live my best life. In living my best life, I will allow the joy of the Lord to fill my heart, mind, and soul. God promised me a husband, and until this time comes, I am grateful Jesus is my bridegroom. I will continue to study the word of God, learning to be steadfast and unmovable, proclaiming the goodness of the Lord to all who need to see and hear.

A song sung by Elevation Worship and Maverick City called Jireh, which states,

"If He dresses the lilies with beauty and splendor, how much more will He clothe you? If He watches over every sparrow, how much more does He love you? Jireh, You are enough!"

"Take the carefree birds as your example… God takes care of every one of them, feeding each of them out of the abundance of his love and goodness. Isn't your life more precious to God than a bird? Be carefree in the care of God!"
~Luke 12:24 (TPT)

God loves me unconditionally; that makes Him enough for me. I will continue to walk this journey with Christ with integrity. He has not steered me wrong yet. His words are confirmed, and His timing is perfect. He chose me to be me, knowing who I was, the mistakes I would make, and the path I would follow, good or bad, and He still chose me. Therefore, I am enough.

I am enough to love again.
I will receive it, believe it, and rejoice in it.
Daughter of a King.

Judgement Day

You, Lord, give perfect peace to those who keep their purpose firm and put their trust in you.

Isaiah 26:3 (GNT)

In the days leading up to our court date, our day of judgment, I began to ask myself, who is this for? Is it for him- the acceptance that his wife no longer wants him? Or is it for me? The closure that I need to move on with the rest of my life. Maybe it's both. I need to know that I survived the storm with all my windows still attached to my house. I need to know that I have made it – I'm worthy, I'm beautiful, I'm smart, and I can survive on my own without the help of a man. I have made it to judgment day, and I can walk confidently and boldly, accepting the fate that lies before me. It's not about money or property- I walk out with my name. The name that I was given at birth and now signifies my rebirth. Na-Tasha Tingman is a born-again creature, and I am content with the thought of that.

Do I still desire a significant other? Of course, I do. I am a human being who loves affection, but through this process, I have learned to love the skin I am in even more and love it without the approval of man. The only approval I need to have is the approval of my Lord and Savior. His opinion of me is the only one that matters the most.

Will I make mistakes? Of course, I will, but my mistakes will not dictate the path I'm destined to walk. It will NOT alter my purpose. If I continue to believe my God will never leave me nor forsake me and believe His promises over my life, there is nothing too hard for my God. He is the provider I will need in my life. He is the regulator of my mind and heart; therefore, my destiny will come forth.

Will I ever love again? Of course, I will, and rightfully so. I'm a Queen who desires her King but will wait for him to be groomed, just as God is grooming me for him. We are destined to be together, and our love will illuminate the love of Christ. As the daughter of a King, I'm destined to be with someone who understands what God brings together; no man, woman, child, or thing can separate what God has ordained. This is the understanding, love, and support I desire, even with all our flaws. Whomever God places in my life, he would know that we will actively pursue and help enlarge our Father's kingdom. What better way to live? Now that's what you call abundant living.

The time has come, and we are sitting across from the judge. When I woke up this morning, I was filled with confidence, and I was ready to face my husband and accept the judgment that was to be handed down on this day. How would I know that anxiety would start to creep in? I was beginning to feel nervous, anxious, and suddenly sad. I looked at my husband, and even though he wasn't going to fight for my love, I was still willing to fight for his.

As many of us should already know, marriage is a two-way street. It contains compromise, communication, and commitment. Knowing whether I am right or wrong, someone will be in my corner while we face the world but will not be afraid to help me get it right in private. It is accepting and embracing all of each other weaknesses and then supporting and building each other up as we climb the ladder to success. As I looked at my husband sitting across from me, facing the judge, I teared up because he couldn't see what was about to happen. He couldn't see he was about to lose one of the only persons in his life that stood by his side through the good and the bad, in sickness and in health. I never let him go to the doctor alone, I never let him go to a game without my support, I never let him go without a hot meal or a clean house, but he wasn't going to fight. I was no longer going to stay bound to someone who couldn't or wouldn't see my worth. That realization is the heartstring that I needed to cut because it hurt so bad. I love that man so much, and I am willing to let go so we can be free from heartache and pain, from the confusion and the non-compromising feuds in our lives. I love that man so much; I am willing to let go because darkness was where he seemed more comfortable. I needed to live in the light, I had to move from the dark, and when I began to move, I couldn't turn back, so everything I loved, if they weren't willing to move with me, had to be left behind.

Instantly, I thought about Lot's wife in the bible. God was destroying Sodom and Gomorrah because of all the darkness it entailed. Abraham interceded on behalf of his nephew Lot and his family to be saved from the destruction. God surrounded me with individuals who interceded on my behalf, and God's will be done in my life and the lives of my family. Amid their escape, Lot's wife looked back and turned to a pillar of salt (Genesis 19:26). She met her demise because she admired, desired, and wished for a life that

God was trying to save her from. As I sat and listened to the judge ask a series of questions to my husband and myself, I couldn't help but thank God for rescuing me from my demise.

Unlike Lot's wife, I was not trying to look back, so I prayed for the strength and peace I would need to continue moving forward to keep running as Lot did from the destruction left behind. Then suddenly, I felt a moment of guilt. I asked myself, *"Is this the right thing to do? Shouldn't I be helping him get over the humps and bumps of life?"* While the judge spoke, I looked over to see that he didn't want to leave the "crap" he built for himself, he was Lot's wife in this scenario, and I was Lot, running for my life. I tried to bring him along, but he kept looking back; he kept living in the past, and moving forward didn't seem like an option. When I came to, the judge stated that we were granted our divorce based on the presented evidence. I can resume my life under my birth name Na-Tasha Tingman.

A tear streamed down my face. I survived it. I was granted the strength to overcome this obstacle, but the peace wasn't quite there. It wasn't until we left the courthouse. We were going down the steps, I turned and looked behind me to see my ex-husband taking his time coming down the stairs, and prophetically I saw he was blind. My ex-husband couldn't see, and it was no longer in my heart; he wouldn't see, but he couldn't see… HE WAS BLIND. At that moment, the peace of God rested over me. I did all I could to keep my marriage; I went through all these emotions because I was uncertain if I was loved, but now I know he cares, but he couldn't see how to love.

I know this may seem rhetorical, or maybe even dumb to some people, many of us stay in a situation thinking we can change someone. If they are not willing to change, should you be responsible for staying in that situation even if it means that you "die"? I have contemplated that question for over a year and a half, and I've concluded that nothing is more important than my salvation and relationship with Christ. A relationship that I'm not quite ready to lose. I will make mistakes, but I will turn to God for the answers on how to make it right, My ex-husband was my heart, and he was tied to my soul by marriage. I have and would have continued to do anything for him. Still, I realized my destiny and purpose are more important to me, and frankly, I just wasn't ready to "die." So, before I left him at the courthouse, I expressed my love and thankfulness for all he has done for me during the past eleven years of my life. I have grown, and I'm thankful for his part in my growth.

Will I ever love again? When I lay in bed with peace and joy in my heart, I will be able to love again. As long as I rise in the morning, I will be able to love again. As long as I wake with a new day of mercy and grace, I will be able to love again. As long as I know that God is by my side, I will be able to love again. I walked away with my head held high, with peace and joy in my heart. I am free, and I will walk in my freedom. Now I ask, God, what is next?

My Revelation:

"Do not be afraid or discouraged for the Lord God; my God is with you. He will not fail you or forsake you."
~1 Chronicle 28:20 (NIV)

God always guides us through the rapids of change. I remember the first time I went parasailing and jet-skiing; it was a terrifying first-time experience; at least that's what I thought. It was a change that I'd never been through before, but I remained strong and courageous; I began to forget about my insecurities, uncertainties, and fears. I began to own the moment with every breath as we began to sail the ocean. I began to possess the moment and just continued to go for it. I realized at that moment that I was a survivor and a conqueror. I could do anything if I just believed.

I didn't know who God was, but I realized that even while I was a citizen of the world, He was always with me, guiding me and protecting me. God was willing and ready to pull me out of what the world expected of me and become the woman He wanted me to be. Now, how wonderful God has been in my life since I have opened my heart and eyes to Him.

Shortly after that, I made another choice that changed my life forever. I moved away from my home, family, and comfort zone to embark on a new journey, which was way scarier than getting on that jet-ski or boat to parasail. As we go through different phases in life, we will embark on difficult choices, just like my separation and divorce. Through it all, if we remain strong and courageous, we can withstand it all.

I say all of this to remind you and me that we will have our fair share of transitions in life. Some we may accept, and some we will not. Some will feel good, and some will not. Changes can kill us or make us stronger, but God will always be on our jet-ski with us through all of life's transitions. He will never leave us alone. Keep your eyes and heart on God. He will navigate the way. Let him navigate you through the sky, waters, sunny days, and the storms. He will bring forth joy and security. He has guided many others through before. He will carry you through as well.

Another revelation that was pertinent to my daily walk in my new life; during my grief, I've tried to find the answer to the question "WHY?" It is something that many of us do, I noticed. I was not alone in that revelation.

Let me talk about me for a minute - I wanted to know Why? Why? Why? Then I've realized in my questioning of Why? Was I more focused on finding the answers to the question than trying to walk through the healing of My Why? It was tiring me out. It takes an abundance of energy to go through the storm as it is (and with the strength of the Lord, we can overcome anything) to add more onto your plate of trying to figure out something our minds are just too minute to figure out. When going through a separation, divorce, or the loss of anything, my advice to myself and anyone it can assist, allow yourself time to go through the emotions. Remember weeping endures for only a night, but JOY comes in the morning. Scripture says, we walk THROUGH the valley of the shadow of death, which means we are never meant to stay there. Both phrases mention the storm as well as the triumph. Once you go through the storm with the help of the Lord, you will receive your revelation of your Why? When the sky begins to clear. Ultimately, the reason behind the storms is usually why you are still here – God wants you to live according to YOUR purpose (God's Purpose). God will never put more on you than you can bear. Whether physical, financial, spiritual, or whatever changes you endure, any transformation requires a sacrifice. Let us continue to allow God to be there with us; He will commune with us, sit with us, sup with us, and in some cases – carry us, even in the storm, because He understands what we are going through.

Live Life Abundantly – Live Free!
It's who you are meant to be.

Are You Willing?

Are you willing to accept a gift so pure that the air we breathe brings life to the bones of our very being?

Are you willing to accept a gift so true that grace and mercy plead your case for you? No matter what you do.

Are you willing to accept a gift of love that, as you enter a room full of darkness, your light shines through?

Are you willing to accept the promises that were made to you for generations to come? All you really need to do is have faith that they shall come true.

No one in the world can speak to a storm, and it will calm down. No one in the world can speak to a mountain, and it shall be moved. No one in this world is capable of changing me into the me I'm destined to be. There is no one.

No one in the world loves unconditionally, sacrificing His only Son for the likes of a sinner like me. There is no one in this world.

I'm willing to:
- Love the one who loves me, despite my flaws
- Love the one who pleads my case, even when I am wrong.
- Love the one who has forgiven all my sins, with hopes I don't do them again.

Oh! How I love Him so.
He has so much in store for me.
He believes in me that I shall see again.

He causes me to confess my sins and is willing to chastise me if I do it again.
He captivates my every thought and softens my heart from every strife.
He continues to PUSH me into this new being;
He stays in the business of freeing-
My heart, my soul, my mind
He does it with grace, and He's not pressed for time.

I love this man that forgives, values, and restores
He desires to help you walk through the many open doors,
He has set aside for you,
while praise and victory continue to be your breakthrough.

I love this man that forgives, values, and restores
Are you willing to sacrifice your flesh for what He has in store?
His eternal life; God of a breakthrough.

I Am Willing, Are You?

Heartfelt Thank-You

Upon completion of this project, one of the most devastating life-changing events happened in my life. God has called home one of His most faithful servants, Dr. Brenda Gary Patterson, affectionately known to many as "Mama Brenda." Even though she never physically gave birth to me, I affectionately called her "Mama" for twelve years. Mama Brenda met my daughter and me and saw something I never saw in myself, HOPE, LOVE, and SALVATION.

Mama Brenda demonstrated through her life what it meant to live as Christ did. She showed what it meant to stand on the Word of God. Mama demonstrated compassion, generosity, humility, faithfulness, amongst many other things. Still, most importantly, it was her LOVE that drew me to her even more. She met me in my place of hurt, confusion, brokenness, bitterness, and anger, and she loved me through it all. She never once gave up on me, and for this, there is no amount of words that could ever express my gratitude to her. I truly thank God for His angel that He has set on earth to push me, motivate me, and love me through it all. Thank You, Father, for allowing your angel to walk with me, talk, edify, laugh, and love me. Thank You, Father, for allowing your angel to instill Your Truth into my soul. Father, Your word was life to Mama, and through her love for You, I was able to witness the life-changing Word of God become life in my very own life.

> *"So, I give you a new commandment: Love each other just as much as I have loved you. For when you demonstrate the same love I have for you by loving one another, everyone will know that you're my true followers."*
>
> *John 13:34-35 (TPT)*

Through this commandment, I knew Mama Brenda was Yours. I knew you must have loved me, and I was born with a Purpose because she poured out that love daily to my daughter and me. Mama prayed without ceasing on my behalf and behalf of my daughter. She stood in the gap for me when I didn't know how to stand in the gap for myself, and once again, Father, I say Thank You.

> *"If your faith remains strong, even while surrounded by life's difficulties, you will continue to experience the untold blessings of God! True happiness comes as you pass the test with faith and receive the victorious crown of life promised to every lover of God!"*
>
> *James 1:12 (TPT)*

Lord, Mama's faith remained strong, and I'm rejoicing in knowing that she has gained her crown of glory and sitting alongside her Father. I'm rejoicing in knowing that to be absent from the body is to be present with the Lord (2 Corinthians 5:8). I'm rejoicing in knowing Jesus, You are the resurrection and the life; and whoever believes in You, (Mama believed in You), shall live (John 11:25). I'm rejoicing because now I know the earth has no sorrow that heaven can't heal (Isaiah 35:10).

Father, I want to share this heartfelt Thank-You for loving me so much; you allowed my paths to cross with Mama Brenda. I love her, and I will forever hold a special place in my heart for her. I pray that all she has instilled in me will bear fruit as you continue to water those same seeds she has planted—Thank-You, Father, for the life of Dr. Brenda Gary Patterson.

I will continue to pray for her children and her family; Lord, You touch them in their time of need. Father, You are the mother to the motherless, so be with them right now. Wrap your arms around them, Father. May the memories that they have of their mother become joy to their hearts. May the memories they have of her laughter bring peace to their soul. May the love she has demonstrated to others be the love they will continue to exhibit, and I pray that it soothes their aching hearts. Hold on to them, Father, and never let them go.

In Jesus Name,
Amen

The Mother of Many

We shed a tear today
Understanding that you couldn't stay
To be absent in the body is to sit in glory with the King
So, we rejoice for all the wisdom you bring
The Mother of Many,
You've touched many souls
You showed all of us unconditional love.

A woman of faith is who you were,
You've extended your heart to many,
That was broken and didn't know where to start.
You planted the seeds and prayed us through,
And watched vigorously at what God would do,
Your arms were strong for the task,
To grow the Kingdom just as God planned.
His faithful servant is who you'll always be,
So, the angels of heaven shall sing praises
When they see you dancing before the pearly gates;
To receive your crown of glory.

You are the epitome of how a godly woman should behave
You spoke wisdom with love, correction lovingly slid off your tongue
And you never backed down until the job was done.
Giving glory to the Father because victory has been won.
You've extended your arms of hope to the poor and bleak,
And shared a meal with anyone that needed to eat.

The Mother of many is who you were,
You moved with strength, grace, and dignity.
You laughed in the face of adversity
Never hiding the Proverbs 31 woman you were called to be.

We shed a tear today
Understanding you couldn't stay
We love you and still wish you were here
But we're rejoicing and singing with you, Mama Brenda
You are home with the Almighty King.

About the Author

Na-Tasha Rise was born Natasha Tingman in Brooklyn, New York. She is the mother of an amazing, intelligent, and determined young woman who is completing her academic career at North Carolina Agriculture & Technology (NCA&T). Na-Tasha is considered by many a mother, sister, and friend. Many also know her to be a woman after God's own heart, walking into her life's purpose.

Na-Tasha has worn many hats during her life, from a Customer Service Representative, Certified Nursing Assistant, Little League Co-Director and Coach, Educator, and now CEO/Publisher of Gift From Above Publishing, LLC. Na-Tasha has dedicated her life to helping others excel. Her daily motto is, *"What kind of day did I have if I didn't help someone smile? Let's make every day a great day to smile."* It just takes a smile to motivate her throughout the day.

Na-Tasha Rise loves to have fun, and her personality says it all. She has never met a stranger; she loves and adores people. She is a mother to many thanks to her previous students, teen girls, and little league athletes, amongst all the young people whose paths she crossed.

One of her most significant accomplishments, besides being a mother, is being the Founder of SC Precious Jewels, a teen girls empowerment program. Established in 2013 to provide young ladies with an opportunity to grow socially and personally, SC Precious Jewels embraces the nature of young ladies. It encompasses community service, leadership development, etiquette workshops, and social activities. SC Precious Jewels help create lifestyle changes that young ladies can use for the duration of their lives. SC Precious Jewels is a sisterhood, a place a young lady can call her own.

As CEO/Publisher of Gift From Above Publishing, LLC, she has reached another plateau in life. Na-Tasha and Gift From Above focuses on elevating, motivating, and inspiring other authors to LIFTT (Love, Inspire, Faith, Teach, Truth) their voices while sharing their Gift From Above with the world.

"Every gift God freely gives is good and perfect, streaming down from the Father of lights, who shines from the heavens…." ~James 1:17 (TPT)

Na-Tasha had fully committed her life to Christ in 2019 when she joined a prayer group called Unwavering Faith International Outreach Ministry. During their 5 am prayers, Na-Tasha had encounter after encounter that shaped and molded her into the woman of integrity that stands up right now. Even though her journey is nowhere near over, she keeps her hands to the plow, so she can continue to see God's glory in her life and those attached to her.

Na-Tasha Rise as a mother:
My mother is one of the bravest, strongest women known to men. She makes the ultimate sacrifices to make sure I'm happy, no matter what it is, and she loves me unconditionally. She would always

speak wisdom and knowledge, no matter the situation. She's constantly reminding me about how I'm destined for greatness, and to be honest with you, I can't be destined for something so significant without my mother by my side. She has such a beautiful soul, and with her kind and caring heart, she is simply perfect for me. God knew exactly what He was doing when He chose us to be mother and child. We're connected as if we are twins, and she's my best friend. I Love her so much.

Xzasha Thomas

Na-Tasha Rise as a daughter:
Who is Na-Tasha Rise to me? Well, let's see, she's my oldest daughter. She was born on February 21, 1979, 6lbs 6 ounces. A tiny baby with two front teeth and ready-to-eat steak. Later, they had to remove them because her teeth were too loose. You wouldn't believe that she still has those tiny teeth in her mouth to this day. Her Blessing! I was young, and yes, I was scared! My mother guided me the first few weeks of her life.

Na-Tasha is a special child; she always wants things her way, especially with her father (he spoiled her a little). I noticed at an early age, Na-Tasha would be a writer and a poet. She always wrote poetry ever since the 4th or 5th grade. Her imagination could go far; it's incredible. She's a brilliant and beautiful woman. She's kind-hearted and always willing to help others, and an amazing mother to her daughter.

From mother to daughter, always shoot for the stars; you could go exceptionally far. Just be consistent in all things that you do, don't give up, and don't let anybody get in the way of your dreams. Stay Positive. Always put God first.

Love Always, Mother

N.T. Orr as a granddaughter:
Na-Tasha is my first granddaughter. When I went to see her for the first time, the shock was that Na-Tasha was the first baby at Kings County Hospital to be born with two front teeth at the top. I thought

her mother had forgotten her toothbrush, only to find out it was needed for Na-Tasha. They were removed before coming home. Babies born with one or more teeth are called Natal Teeth, which is as rare as Na-Tasha. I realized then that she will be chewing her way through life. That is just what she has done.

Natasha has a love for reading, bubble baths with music, and grandma's weekends. Summer months were spent with me... going shopping and cooking together, which explains her love of cooking different dishes and shopping. Na-Tasha still calls me at times for recipes when she thinks she has forgotten something. So, world, I introduce to you My Na-Tasha!

Love Grandma Audrey

www.ingramcontent.com/pod-product-compliance
Lightning Source LLC
Chambersburg PA
CBHW051450290426
44109CB00016B/1698